PRAISE F

'A tour de force . . . funny, committed and impassioned'
GoodReads

'A playful, powerful page-turner . . . a brilliant
blend of memoir and travel writing'
LoveReading

'Intelligent, warm-hearted, down-to-earth
and often very funny. *Ganbatte!*'
Alan Spence

'A gently quirky memoir'
Canberra Times

'A warm, funny, joyful experience'
Country Life

'A treasure . . . written with affection, insight and a lot of humour'
Sorted

'A perfect read for the novice of Japanese
culture . . . bold, humorous and current'
Japan Society

'This book is guaranteed to make you laugh, but its emotional
moments hit hard and by the end, you'll feel like you've made a friend'
SavvyTokyo.com

'A delightful tumble into village life, complete with a vivid
cast of characters and a beautiful sense of place'
The Scotsman

The Only Gaijin in the Village

Iain Maloney

First published in Great Britain in 2020 by
Polygon, an imprint of Birlinn Ltd.
This paperback edition published in 2021 by Polygon.

Birlinn Ltd
West Newington House
10 Newington Road
Edinburgh
EH9 1QS

www.polygonbooks.co.uk

1

ISBN 978 1 78027 739 4

British Library Cataloguing-in-Publication Data
A catalogue record for this book is available on
request from the British Library.

Typeset by Biblichor Ltd, Edinburgh

Contents

Summer

Autumn

Winter

Spring

夏

Summer

Yes, I Am a Long Way From Home

I'm going to die in Japan.

At least, that's the plan. Plan is the wrong word. I've not sat down like Wile E. Coyote gripped by a wave of self-destruction and plotted my own demise, strung an anvil from the roof or painted a tunnel on the garage door. Nor am I predicting that a North Korean missile will take me out any time soon, though that is certainly more likely. I have the experience to prove it. It was 29 August 2017.

I was camping in Aomori, the most northerly prefecture on Honshu, Japan's main island. Over the water is Hokkaido – the last prefecture before Russia – then a string of disputed islands and ice. During the summer vacation I'd thrown the camping gear in the back of the car, caught up in a surge of wild-man envy. I needed masculine exploits and rugged scenery. By the time I'd reached Aomori I'd already been stung thirty-six times by bees, developed a fever as a result, been chased by a biker gang and run away from a hotel before they discovered that when my fever broke I'd sweated so much I'd turned their comfortable mattress into a water bed. I'd been travelling for ten days, hadn't spoken to anyone for three, and was beginning to crack up. I woke about 4 a.m., packed up quickly, happy to have been undisturbed by bears, and pointed the car south. Mogwai soared from the open windows as I sped through glorious forest roads – the kind Iain Banks called 'great wee roads' – with the sun rising behind me.

I joined the highway a little before six, my intention to go as far as Sendai, refuel and take it from there. A night in the city or another campsite? Fresh sheets or the pleasure of a lakeside sunset? My phone, acting as a sat nav from the 100-yen holster I'd taped to the dashboard, started buzzing like thirty-six bees had got inside it, immediately followed by a screeching alarm, far louder than the ear-hurting stereo volume. It was the J-Alert.

J-Alert is a nationwide warning system designed with two functions: the first is to give people a few seconds' notice in advance of an earthquake or other disaster. (A few seconds is all science can give us, but it can make a lot of difference. It can be enough time to turn off the gas cooker, to get away from the windows, to get out the shower and avoid the indignity of running from the house in soapy humiliation.) The second is to scare the living shit out of people. With a volume and tone similar to the 'howler' letters in Harry Potter – think an air horn attached to a bull horn being held down by someone intent on giving you a heart attack – the J-Alert has caused me to leap from bed in the small hours, stub a toe, crack a shin, hit my head and fall to the floor in terror. This time it caused me to swerve wildly into the outside lane. Luckily the highway was empty. Had it not been, I wondered, would my death count as an earthquake fatality? In Australia, most deaths caused by spiders have nothing to do with bites and industrial levels of venom. Rather, the majority of fatalities are caused by people pulling down the sun visor while cruising along innocently, having a dangerous spider fall into their lap, very naturally reacting with some surprise and crashing the car into a wall/truck/convincing picture of a tunnel left by Wile E. Coyote. Spiders don't kill people, I'm sure the NRA would say, walls do.

The alarm finished, I righted my direction and pulled back into the inside lane. Japanese highways are raised affairs. Literal highways on massive concrete legs with high sides to keep the noise in and presumably to stop any spider-surprised drivers from going over the edge. During the 1995 earthquake, the raised highway in Kobe flipped over. If there was a big earthquake, I wanted to be somewhere less . . . flippable. I wanted to be on a great wee road, ideally in Scotland.

After the alarm, an electronic female voice announced in Japanese, 'MISSILE LAUNCH! MISSILE LAUNCH!'

'What?'

'MISSILE LAUNCH! MISSILE LAUNCH!'

'I thought that's what you said.'

I pulled the phone from its slot and tried to read the alert. In Japanese. In a tiny font. Still doing about 100kph on the highway. Not bright but, you know, special circumstances.

Missile launch! Missile launch! Get to a safe place. Find somewhere underground or go inside a strong building.

High in the air, on a concrete strip. The next exit was 20km away.

No further information from the J-Alert. I went onto Twitter. The alert was already trending but every tweet was a variation of 'WTF?'. I phoned Minori, my wife.

'What?'

'What's happening?'

'I'm asleep.'

'No, with the missile.'

'What missile?'

'The alert.'

'Are you drunk?'

'Put on the news and call me back.'

As I waited I remembered that the day before, driving north, I'd been stuck behind a convoy of military vehicles. Trucks, jeeps, and something that looked so suspiciously like a rocket launcher that I took a photo. For about thirty minutes I'd trailed this convoy. I'd assumed there was a base nearby, though the surprised expressions and pointed fingers of villagers made me suspect not. They'd turned off a few kilometres before my junction and I'd thought no more about it. Now the presence of that rocket launcher seemed ominous. Did they know something?

'Hi. Where are you?'

'On the highway in Aomori. What's going on?'

'The TV says it's a test.'

'North Korea?'

'Of course. It flew over Hokkaido and landed in the sea.'

She had this tone like it was the most mundane thing in the world. Like she was reciting the weather forecast or responding to me telling her about my day.

'So we're not at war?'

'Not yet. What are your plans?'

'I was going to go to Sendai. Now I'm not so sure.'

'Okay. Drive safe.'

'Let me know if a war starts.'

'Okay.'

As I drove south I pondered my situation. If war did break out, what would I do? In many ways I was already in the best place. I was in the middle of nowhere, or at least very close to it, with enough provisions to last a week, maybe two if I was careful. I had a car full of camping gear, water, food fresh and dried. But I was a long way from home. What would I do? Should I make a dash for home or hole up in the forest and wait it out? Scenes from various post-apocalyptic films played out. Soon I was imagining a zombie infestation and making plans.

By 10 a.m. I'd reached Sendai. I came off the highway and refuelled. I was exhausted, stiff, itchy and sore, and now Kim was lobbing missiles at me. The holiday was over. Time to go home.

In twelve hours I drove more than 1,000 kilometres, stopping at service stations for lunch and dinner. When I swung into the driveway, I felt all the tension seep away.

I was home. This is where I want to die. Home is where the heart stops.

It was my neighbour who first made me think about it in this way. He asked me outright not long after we bought the house. We were sitting in my garden with a beer each and the conversation quickly ran beyond getting-to-know-you inanities. In his forties, he was still living in the house he'd been born in and will remain there until he dies, his son taking over mastership. Such is the Japanese way, and so common is it that it often never occurs to some that there could be an alternative. So when a foreigner bought the house next door, Kensuke seemed at a loss to understand why. Surely at some point I'd go home? Only soldiers and refugees died in foreign lands. And if so, why buy a house and a big plot of land? Why not rent somewhere far more convenient until it was time to leave? It wasn't xenophobia or anything like that, no 'when are you going home?' enquiry that can be expressed by some in Japan. Rather, it was just an idea so far beyond his experience and desires that he felt he had to tackle it head on.

'You're going to live here until you die?'

'That's the plan.'

I moved to Japan from Scotland in 2005. Sometime in 2013, Minori and I decided to decamp from our Aichi commuter town. We both grew up in the countryside and the idea of space, of greenness, of silence and solitude resonated like a temple bell. We contacted a *fudō-san* (an estate agent) and explained our plan.

'So where do you want to buy a house?'

'We don't care, as long as it's rural.'

'But close to your jobs?'

'No, we're going to get new ones.'

'Okay. But somewhere convenient?'

'No, we don't care about convenience.'

He twirled his pen and looked at us, baffled by this un-Japanese concept. 'So what are your criteria?'

'Beautiful.'

'Quiet.'

'Big. We want to grow our own vegetables.'

'You want to be farmers? Oh, in that case –'

'No, just enough to support ourselves.'

'Okay, but the house. Do you want –'

'We don't care about that either. It's the land that matters.'

He threw his pen down in defeat, clearly a man who had never seen *The Good Life*. He mulled, hummed, pondered the ceiling. 'You know what? My job's getting pretty boring. This sounds like a new challenge. I'm in.'

In Japan a house is for life, not just for Christmas. In the most seismically active country in the world, houses depreciate in value as soon as you drive them off the forecourt. The land usually appreciates – land is limited in a predominantly mountainous country – though an ageing population and a well-publicised disinterest in the reproductive arts amongst young people mean that even the price of land is sure to fall. But houses aren't built to last. The older a house is, the more likely it is for an earthquake to shake, rattle and roll it. With houses as with TV demographics, anything over about twenty is considered irrelevant to the market.

Consequently, there is no housing market of which to speak. Second-hand houses here have the same reputation as second-hand cars in the UK. Low mileage, one careful owner, but make sure you get someone who knows what they're doing to look under the hood. People buy new-builds or, if they can afford it, order to their tastes. If you decide to move on, your property will not only be worth less than you paid for it, it might be practically unsellable. The new owners would have to factor in the cost of demolishing the old house before they begin paying for their own home, rendering it massively unattractive. Add VAT on everything and you've got the kind of dead property market that would clear immigration off the *Daily Mail*'s front page for months.

There is no property ladder. You can't start small and build up to your dream home. When you buy, you buy for life. So you'd better get it right first time. You'd better be damn sure you know what you're doing. No buyer's remorse here. Hence Kensuke's confusion.

Three years after first meeting the *fudō-san*, in May 2016, we got the keys to a house in Gifu Prefecture. It wasn't as rural as we first imagined – we have neighbours, and it's only a twenty-minute drive to the nearest supermarket – but it's a small community and we're on the edge of it, surrounded by trees, seemingly cut off. It was idyllic and we were delighted.

That lasted about thirty hours.

As I drove back and forth from our old apartment with boxes, bikes and bedding, Minori and her parents cleaned the new house, hung curtains and unpacked. While I was away the *hanchō-san*, the head of the neighbourhood association (where the phrase 'head honcho' comes from), Sasaki-san, and our immediate neighbour, Asai-san, appeared and introduced themselves.

This is how my wife relayed it to me later: 'After introducing themselves they started complaining about the trees. They want us to cut three down because the leaves block their gutters every autumn. They were so rude about it.'

She was nearly in tears, the stress of the move now combined with this. I was angry, but it was night already and there was little I could do about it. We went to bed worried that we'd made a terrible mistake.

There were two main issues we were concerned about before buying the house. I was worried about racism. We were told by one owner that he wouldn't sell to a foreigner. There had been another place our *fudō-san* told us not to buy because while driving through the village he'd seen two huge black trucks covered with flags and imperial regalia driving around blasting nationalistic music and anti-foreign slogans. Not what you want in the next driveway. It's a cliché but rural communities are often resistant to incomers, and foreign incomers are usually even less welcome.

Minori was worried about the neighbourhood association. She quickly tires of the rules and responsibilities Japanese society foists upon its citizens. The idea of attending meetings, standing guard over garbage collection sites and having to listen to the never-ending complaints of elderly people with nothing better to do filled her with dread and loathing. Neighbours are troublemakers, and here, she'd been proven right.

The next day I saw Asai in his garden and marched across to introduce myself. After the standard pleasantries and *onegaishimasu*-es (a greeting/polite expression with no English equivalent) and *your Japanese is very good*-s, I broached the subject.

'My wife tells me there's a problem with the trees. Don't worry, we'll deal with them, but can you give us a bit of time? We haven't even unpacked yet.'

'Problem? What problem?'

'She says you want us to cut these three trees down.'

'No! Don't cut these down. They're cherry blossom trees, they're so beautiful in the spring. Please don't cut them!'

'So what's the problem?'

'Nothing. I was just explaining to her that these trees are mine, and I'll look after them. Those ones are yours, and they're your responsibility. Look, the land boundary runs down here.'

We laughed at the misunderstanding, at the fact that the native Japanese speaker had misunderstood while the foreigner with the broken Japanese and weird accent had sorted it out. His son, Kensuke, came over with three beers. We *kampai*-ed, and they gave me a lesson in Japanese dendrology. Asai left, and Kensuke sat down with me, leading to the 'Are you going to live here until you die?' question. He and I both meant decades hence, at the end of a full and natural lifespan. I didn't imagine that my continued existence would be so comprehensively threatened by Kim Jong-Un, snakes or typhoons over the next year.

Who by Fire

The first rule of living in Japan is: show willingness.

While Asai didn't have a problem with the trees overhanging his land, the bushes by the road were another thing. The previous owner had let these coniferous triffids grow like slow green fireworks, spreading crystalline in every direction, to the point where they were in danger of scratching passing cars on the narrow single-track road. Sasaki, the *hanchō*, made his position on shrubbery clear.

'I asked him on numerous occasions to cut them. He never did.' A sad shake of the head. The very idea that someone could be so unwilling to do what was needed for the good of the community. I suspect Sasaki was a salesman in his working days, or maybe a politician. He certainly has a touch of the Machiavellian.

'I understand.' The most loaded words in Japanese. Not just 'I get what you're saying' but 'I fully understand the unspoken nuance and the implications'. As foreigners, *wakarimashita* – I understand – and its negation, *wakarimasen*, are problematic terms. I was once involved in a small scuffle outside a football ground when an opposition fan incorrectly believed me to have emptied my beer over the back of his jacket. Unaware that, as a Scotsman, the very idea was anathema, we argued for a few minutes. I had no idea what he was talking about and said so, in Japanese: *I've no idea what you're talking about.*

'Oh, now he's pretending he can't speak Japanese.'

'No, obviously I can speak Japanese. We're speaking Japanese. Listen, I'm speaking Japanese now. That doesn't mean I can understand your nonsense.'

'See, he's doing it again.'

Surprise is often expressed that anyone other than the Japanese can speak the language, so when a foreigner says, 'I don't understand,' then it's necessarily a linguistic issue and not the fact that your interlocutor is a drunk football fan talking shite. It can be a touch frustrating.

No such trouble with Sasaki. He understands. We bow. He wanders off to take a piss behind his garage. He seems to like the spot. Every once in a while I'll pass by to see him emerging, doing himself up. I guess when you reach that age, you just can't hold on.

I go inside. 'I need your dad's help. Does he have a chainsaw?'

'What for?'

'Sasaki –'

'Was he peeing again?'

'Yes, but it's not for that. We need to deal with those bushes. A trim won't do it. We need to take them right back.'

'I'll call him.'

While she does I go back outside. I'm still trying to get the feel of it. This is my garden, my place. I can't just let my gaze drift over the natural beauty of it. I'm responsible for every atom of it. The land is more or less rectangular, with the house in the south-east corner, a few metres in from the boundary. Behind the house, next to Sasaki's land, is something of a dead area. A long strip covered by anti-weed sheets, a couple of trees and nothing else. What to do with this? What to do with any of it? What the hell am I going to do with half an acre? There's only two of us. How many potatoes are we going to need? How many potatoes can two people reasonably eat before they become sick of potatoes?

Sasaki's land stops in parallel with my bathroom and the rest, up to the road, is home to Hasegawa-san. There's a persimmon tree in the corner, and more of the coniferous bastards running along the boundary. Inside my land, behind these bushes, is a second level of foliage, like a line of archers behind the infantry. It more or less makes this end of the land impenetrable. Pushing between them leaves one peppered in sticky seeds, cobwebs and stuff that itches. However, the whole thing acts as a buffer between the house and the rest of the world. No need for net curtains. Any peeping Tom trying to get a glimpse of me watching

Game of Thrones in my underpants is going to have to Indiana Jones his way through with a machete first. I wade into the undergrowth to get an idea of what we're dealing with, scratches and itches starting up almost immediately.

'Maloney-san? Maloney-san?'

I push my way towards the voice, which I suspect is Hasegawa. Ducking under the low-hanging branches of the persimmon tree, I find her standing beside her silver Suzuki. Hasegawa is in her seventies, tiny but made entirely of steel. She lives alone, her husband having passed on and her son having relocated to Chiba for university decades before and never returned. The Suzuki, I later learn, doesn't move. She's too nervous to drive these days, and the dent in the side fender and scratches along the doors suggests she may be wise not to.

'Hasegawa-san, how are you?'

'Tired. Always tired. Sasaki-san asked you to cut the hedges.'

I had understood. 'Yes, my father-in-law is bringing a chainsaw, and then we'll tidy the place up.'

'While you're at it, do you think you could bring these bushes under control as well? Just that they're getting a bit big, blocking out the light. It's hard to dry my clothes.'

'No problem. All of these ones?'

'Yes. I asked the previous owner but . . .'

I'm beginning to think not everyone was sad to see the back of him.

'As soon as I can get the chainsaw, we'll get to work. Please be a little patient but I'll definitely do it.'

The next day my father-in-law turns up with the chainsaw. He shows me how to use it, explains where the petrol goes, the chain oil. How to stand, how to hold it. I nod along. *Wakarimashita.*

Yoji looks at me, at the chainsaw. 'Which bushes?'

I show him. 'All along the road and then next to Hasegawa's house.'

He looks at me, at the chainsaw. 'I'll do it.'

'No, it's okay, I can manage.'

He looks at me, at the chainsaw. 'No.'

I turn to Minori.

'He's like that. Doesn't trust anyone not to fuck up. It's not you.'

'It feels like it's me.'

'Just let him do it.'

'Do I have any choice?'

'It's his chainsaw.'

To be fair to him, he's very good with the chainsaw. Could probably do art with it if he were inclined that way. My role is to drag fallen branches aside and pile them in the garden. Shorts and a T-shirt were a mistake. I quickly resemble a self-loathing Emo teenager or the owner of the worst cat in the world. A crowd begins to gather: Asai and his wife, Junko, the man from across the road, Ishikawa and two of his three daughters, Sasaki and his wife Michiko, and Hasegawa. Between the buzzing and shrieking they comment on Yoji's skill with the saw, at how quickly I'm clearing up, at how much I'm starting to bleed.

For some unfathomable reason each bush has electrical wire wrapped round it. Clearly it's been there for a while; some of it is embedded in the trunk where the bush has grown around it. It causes problems for the chainsaw, for Yoji, as he tries to avoid metal-on-metal action. A pile of wire in plastic coating builds up. This is the first inkling we get that the previous owner had some idiosyncratic ways of maintaining his property.

A car passes, so we stop and scatter. Another. A third, this one stops. It's Minori's aunt and uncle. They can't get into the drive because it's full of severed bush. I point out I had no idea they were coming. The uncle looks at me expectantly, so I clear the driveway for him.

In Japan, the first rule of fitting in is showing willingness.

Tea appears, juice, snacks. Yoji and I keep working. Picnic chairs are produced. We keep at it. We reach the end of the road and Yoji refills the tank.

'These ones?'

'Yeah.'

'Cut them the same as the ones on the road?'

I look at the bushes, and the second row of bushes behind them. Where Hasegawa hangs her washing. 'Take them out.'

'Completely?'

'Yeah. It'll take less time and we won't have to worry about them again.'

'All right.'

He goes along the line slicing them a couple of inches off the ground. I disappear into their razor branches as I haul them – each one the size of a couple of Christmas trees taped together – out of the way so that finally my face resembles the rest of my body. Hasegawa is over the moon. Mutterings of contentment ripple through the assembled throng. I have shown willingness, I have done my duty above and beyond what was expected. I have literally bled for them. I have spilled blood on the ground to please my new neighbours. I have earned some slack, some approval.

Approval from everyone except Minori.

'You're not coming into the house like that. Wash the blood and filth off.'

'How?'

'Hose.'

More of Minori's relatives arrive, buoyed by the chance to have a nose around the house. Her brother, his wife and three kids show up carrying beer and snacks. Divested of greenery and scabbing nicely, beer seems ideal. It is a beautiful May afternoon in the middle of Golden Week, a period of close-packed national holidays and one of the few occasions when put-upon Japanese workers can take some time off. Everyone is in holiday humour. A quick confab and a barbecue is decided upon. Minori and her mum shoot off to buy meat, while I get the fire going.

I'm a big fan of barbecues. Coming from the North East of Scotland, they were few and far between, and a sure sign of a special occasion. My father feels the same and can be credited with the invention of a new type of barbecue: the sarcastic barbecue.

My dad is the eldest of five children, the other four being women. The eldest of these, Kathleen, emigrated to Australia. At least once in every generation, one Maloney decides that the only thing that can hold us all together is extreme distance and sods off to the other side of the planet. Perhaps it's the Scottish/Irish genes in us, a history of emigration, the diaspora, or maybe it's just that some of us fare better out of sight and out of mind. Kathleen married an Aussie, had two sons. One year they came over for Christmas, the day of which was to be held at my dad's house. Christmas dinner was the standard fare but Boxing Day was something different. Fed up with repeated references to the southern hemisphere, Christmas on the beach and barbecues, he decided to give them what they seemed to want. A barbecue. In Aberdeenshire. In winter. After a white Christmas. A sarcastic barbecue.

In my garden, I'd already built a fire pit. There was a half-hearted attempt at one when we moved in, a hole in the ground with a couple of rocks around it, as pathetic as if a group of sloth druids had considered building their nascent civilisation a Stonehenge then given up and climbed into the trees for a good, long hang. I filled that in, planted a pine seedling on top and started again in a more central location, taking advantage of a couple of stone lanterns that had been left behind and a gap in the trees through which we can see Mount Ontake on a clear day. I dragged in three railway sleepers to act as benches, nearly crippling myself in the process, and slowly set about turning the area into what I like to think of as a clearing in the forest of *A Midsummer Night's Dream* but which my wife likes to call 'a pile of nonsense'. I secreted various statuettes of unnamed deities, a couple of Grecian urns and a wooden surfer who looks like a cross between Willem Dafoe's Green Goblin and Eric Trump, in the grass, bushes and trees around the fire pit, and hung two strings of 100 per cent real Tibetan prayer flags I bought from a 100 per cent real Tibetan man in a 100 per cent real Tibetan market in Aberfeldy, Scotland. I think it looks mystical. Kensuke asked me if I was having a sports day.

The barbecue is a success and soon begins attracting the neighbours. The sun sets, we light candles in the stone lanterns and throw more logs on the fire. The Asais join us – the kids climbing in the trees, the adults drinking and chatting. Kensuke's cousin appears with his guitar and plays a few songs. Takahiro is good. Excellent in fact, and plays Clapton's 'Tears In Heaven', fingering both the guitar and vocal parts. Minori tells me to get my guitar out but it is impossible to play along with him. He is one of those virtuoso musicians who doesn't know how to play with others. Where would my guitar fit in? Playing music is about leaving space for each other, listening and collaborating. He is used to playing solo and fills in all the blanks himself. We take turns playing songs the other has never heard of, like the most anti-social karaoke night ever. Minori's family drifts away, Takahiro heads off, and next-door's kids are escorted inside for bath time, leaving me, her, Asai, Kensuke, his brother Kyota and Sasaki. More beers and a rousing version of 'Let It Be'. A voice calls out, and Yamada-san, an elderly man who lives two rice fields away, emerges from the gloaming. Behind him come two men I haven't met. They are introduced as Kagawa-san and Endo-san, both retired. Yamada carries a six-pack, Endo a bottle of *shōchū* and Kagawa has packets of dried squid. Another log on the fire and the party blazes up once more. The guitar is passed over, and Yamada gives us a Japanese version of Dylan's 'Don't Think Twice, It's All Right' in a voice that sounds like he is driving a motorbike over a ploughed field. More beer. More saké. More songs.

This is the life. The lubricant of alcohol and the shared language of music by the fireside, as humans have done for thousands of years.

Our voices raised in song.

Our voices raised in laughter.

Our voices raised . . .

Raised voices?

Kagawa and Endo, each perched on either end of a railway sleeper bench with a wooden statue of Ebisu between them, grinning in the flickering light, are arguing in a language I have yet to master but in which I hope to one day become fluent: drunk-old-man Japanese.

Minori having gone inside, I turn to Kensuke. 'What's the problem?'

'I'm not sure. Something about the war.'

I am on high alert, the Basil Fawlty in me primed. When I first arrived in the country one of the things we were warned about during our brief and woefully inadequate teacher training was to avoid history. As a Scot I tend not to get dragged into historical assumptions the way some of my American friends do. I once got confronted by an irate schoolboy in the Hiroshima Peace Memorial Museum, demanding to know if I was American. Presumably he wanted an explanation and an apology there and then had I turned out to be from Omaha.

'Scotland.'

'Doko?' *Where?*

Kagawa and Endo are up on their feet, gesturing with their cups. What is it? Nanjing? Pearl Harbor? Nagasaki? Comfort women? Any number of contentious issues fly through my mind, and in none of them does the conversation end with hugs all round and recharged glasses. Asai wades in on Kagawa's side, calling Endo an idiot. Sasaki backs up Endo. Everyone over sixty-five is on their feet, the rest of us watching this bizarre theatre unfold in my garden Globe.

Kensuke joins in, contradicting his father. I nudge him. 'In the woods beyond the shrine,' he says, 'there's a war memorial. They're arguing about which war.'

'Who thinks what?'

'Kagawa and that faction think it's the second, Endo says it's the first.'

'Why don't we go and see?' It may be a bit late in the day for pragmatism but that is the only club in my bag.

Kensuke relays my suggestion, and my wife returns from the house in time to see the entire male party – me, Kensuke, Kyota, Kagawa, Endo, Sasaki and Yamada – trailing out of the garden with torches (the electric kind, though if we'd had flaming ones, we'd have used them) and back-up drinks. We zigzag our way around the rice fields towards the shrine. Endo disappears up a tiny stone staircase into the trees and we dutifully follow. Images from my childhood, from *Twin Peaks* and *The Blair Witch Project*, haunt me as we sweep aside branches and pick cobwebs out of our mouths. The air is rich with the hum of insects and the smell of the local *shōchū* wafting from our breath.

'Aha!' Endo stands smugly, his torch dancing over the date. All but forgotten, this stone monument bears only one name, that of the lone local man who died in the First World War. The monument is covered in Imperial flags and patriotic sentiments. Had the dates been two or three decades later, I would've felt less ambivalence but Japan fought on the allies' side in the First World War, taking German colonies off them at the behest of the British. This isn't a political, ideological site like Yasukuni, this is a memorial such as every town in Britain has, remembering the local lads who went to fight in a war that had nothing to do with existential threats and everything to do with geopolitical dick-swinging, and never came back. It isn't there to make a point. It is there to remind. We stand in silence, taking in the melancholy of the moment, before raising our cups and cans and toasting the fallen soldier.

We return to the fireside and finish our drinks. The party broke up soon after, each man fading into the darkness, unsteady on the road.

The Outdoors Type

Japanese people are proud of Japan, which is fair enough. The media overdoes the patriotism a bit, and sometimes that pride can turn into disrespect for other countries, but show me a country that isn't guilty of that. The Japanese have some good reasons to be proud, chief among which is the oft-cited claim that Japan is safe. The mantra is repeated in the news, during welcome ceremonies for overseas workers and any time the government tentatively floats the idea of opening the door to immigrants from a crack to ajar. Japan is safe. People are cognisant of that fact and use it as an excuse not to go overseas. It's safe here, why go somewhere less safe? Japan is safe, and we're going to keep it that way.

If we're talking about crime, then okay. In comparison with many other countries Japan has low crime rates. According to a 2017 Gallup study, Japan ranked 105th out of 110 for incidence of crime. Singapore was 110th since you ask. Petty crime is basically non-existent, if you don't count bicycle theft and dangerous driving (two things the Nagoya area is famous for. *Nagoyabashiri*, Nagoya driver, is the pejorative used for a bad driver). I once drunkenly left my mobile on top of an ATM and found it waiting for me the next morning, something locals find utterly unremarkable. You can generally walk home late at night without fear of mugging, molestation or anything more sinister than a drunk salaryman hoping for a free English lesson. At least men can; I still wouldn't advise a woman to walk home alone at night, though I know many who do without incident. Numbers on sexual assaults are unreliable since few women report them and hardly any are ever prosecuted. There are queries all the way down the line, but your chances of being a victim of crime in Japan are significantly less than in Scotland.

So, Japan is safe, certainly in terms of what fellow humans might do to you. If you throw the net wider, things look less secure. If you don't count earthquakes, tsunamis, active volcanoes, typhoons and the associated frequent landslides, Japan is safe. If you ignore the shaky logic of building forty-three nuclear reactors in the most seismically active country on the planet, Japan is safe. If you turn a blind eye to employment practices that result in *karoshi* – death from overwork – and high suicide rates; if you sweep the problem of the Yakuza and other gangs under the *tatami*; if you don't ask why the hills are alive with the sound of those annoying bells hikers hang from their packs, making summer in Kamikōchi ring like Santa's sleigh, Japan is safe. Bears, wild boar, things that creep and things that crawl. The people may be well behaved but the geology, climate, flora and fauna sure as hell aren't.

My first encounter with a typhoon came by accident. I'd been here less than two months when Francis called up. Francis worked for the same company and had been on the same flight out. On the train to Nagoya, while I kept watch for stations, forcing my eyes open, he slept.

'We're going to climb Fuji.'

'Good for you. When?'

'Tomorrow. Coming?'

'Um. Nope.'

'Come on, the climbing season finishes the day after tomorrow. This could be our only chance.'

'I don't know the first thing about –'

'It's all right, we've got all the details. Just meet us at Nagoya station at seven tomorrow.'

'Sure, why not?'

The next morning I threw some clothes into my backpack, some snacks, my skiing jacket. I only had a beaten pair of Vans but they were hardy and would probably be fine.

Probably.

You're beginning to see where this is going, aren't you?

This was the least prepared-for expedition since Hannibal took his elephants over the Alps and completely forgot to pack sticky buns.

There's only one bus a day from the Shinkansen station to Fuji station 5, where the climb starts. We missed it. Not by a little, by hours. We got a taxi. Halfway there, with the meter at 13,000 yen, the driver took pity on us and switched it off. It still cleaned me out of cash. When we got to station 5 it was late afternoon. The idea was to climb up to watch the sunrise from the summit. What I know now, and none of us knew then, is that you climb up the day before, sleep in the station just below the summit, then climb the last stretch in the minutes before dawn. You don't climb during the night with a weak torch to light the way.

A fog came in. The rain started. The wind got up. Fuji is made of sand so every second step took us backwards. The weather got worse. At one point we took shelter in a cave-like hole under an overhanging rock. At times I suspected we were really climbing Mount Doom. The weather got even worse. We were climbing Fuji during a fucking typhoon. In the least appropriate clothing ever. No one had thought to check the weather. No one had thought to check anything. We made it, somehow, to the final station. It was locked down and you had to pay to stay: we had no money. We found an open door – into the staff quarters, it later transpired – stripped off our soaking clothes and settled down to wait the night out. The storm worsened. We nearly froze. Eventually others woke up, but thankfully just ignored us. Everyone set off for the top. I managed about twenty metres then started collapsing. Altitude sickness. I didn't have the lungs for it. I turned back, letting the others go on, something you should never do. I started walking down and didn't stop until the car park. A Japanese proverb says a wise man climbs Fuji once, a fool climbs it twice. I didn't even make it once but clearly I was a fool.

My first earthquake experience also provided me with an unsought-for chance at humiliation. I was teaching, three students and myself sitting round a table. At first it sounded and felt like a big truck was going past. Then I realised what was going on. I panicked, jumped to my feet. 'It's an earthquake, an earthquake, what do we do? Get under the table? In the doorway? Should we run?'

The students – one businessman, one elderly gentleman and a high-school girl – watched me, waited for a beat to tick by, then burst out laughing.

'It's okay, it's just a small one.'

'A small one?'

'Of course.'

'But my chair moved. It bounced me across the floor.'

The businessman looked me up and down. 'Maybe not so small.'

More laughter. Bastards.

Safe, my arse.

If you don't go outside, it's safe.

If you wrap yourself in bubble wrap, it's safe.

If you don't look under the rocks in my garden, Japan is safe.

Moving into the countryside and becoming an amateur farmer introduced me to a new and unfamiliar concept: I found myself thinking, I know just how Samuel L. Jackson feels.

Snakes. Not on a plane, but hiding in the woodpile, between rocks and, once, in the well.

Japan isn't safe. Scotland is safe. Seismically, Scotland is as active as a teenager at 8 a.m. on a Monday morning. Despite a dirty great fault line running through the country like a samurai's death slash, its geology snoozes deeper than if it had a chemistry test at nine o'clock and had been up until three snapchatting. There are no bears, no wild boar, and the only venomous snake is the adder, so unthreatening it was named after a condescending term for a mathematician.

Japan – and my garden in particular – has the *mamushi,* the brown and beige pit viper with a diamond-shaped head. There are other, more dangerous snakes such as the *habu,* but Chubu is too cold for them. They, like the US armed forces, prefer the warmth of Okinawa. For this, I give thanks. I would far rather be Saint Patrick, patron-sainting over a land free of snakes, than Samuel L. Jackson, battling them.

But, like Jackson, peacefully enjoying his in-flight movie and complimentary nuts, battle sought me out.

Where my land ends and Asai's begins, there are a number of what can only be described as massive boulders. They were placed there by the previous owner's grandfather during a spell of Zen decorating or feng shui rearranging, and very nice they are too. Japanese gardening uses the theory of borrowed landscape, where the garden design incorporates aspects beyond the boundaries to create depth. In this instance, the boulders form a symbiotic relationship with Mount Ontake in the distance. They also harbour *mamushi*.

I am a peaceful man, and usually find myself disagreeing with Paul McCartney's injunction to 'Live And Let Die', preferring the alliterative and far more pacifist formulation. When I first noticed the coil of muscle and the diamond head, I made a deal with it, much as I had with my students: let's just leave each other in relative peace.

However, the *mamushi* is dangerous, particularly to children, and the Asai family have three of them (children, not snakes). So I decided something had to be done. I tried to capture it with the aim of relocating it far from harm, but the snake didn't seem keen on that. It had found a nice spot to rest and considered me something of an unwelcome bailiff. And so it was that, much like a Trump press conference, things quickly took a turn for the worse. Battle commenced.

Nothing in my Scottish upbringing had prepared me for this moment. The closest I'd come to confronting nature head on had been frantically sweeping a mouse out of the kitchen of an Edinburgh flat like a crazed Olympic curler. The closest I'd come to snake bite was in the student union. I donned my armour – wellies and oven gloves – and selected a weapon. In the *janken* of life, it turns out shovel beats snake. I felt horrible but I'd have felt worse if one of the children had died of a snake bite.

In the bonfire I gave it a funeral fit for a Viking chief then texted my wife.

I just killed a mamushi.

What did you do with it?

I cremated it.

My dad's going to be angry.

What? Had I committed some enormous faux pas? Was there some Shinto cleansing ritual that needed to be performed? Some Buddhist rite that would make amends for the murder I had committed? My father-in-law never struck me as a particularly religious or spiritual man but maybe I had underestimated him. Wracked with guilt and more than a little put out that my bravery in selflessly putting myself between harm and the Asai younglings had gone unremarked, I stoked the fire – being far more careful when grabbing wood off the pile than I hitherto had been – and waited to get told off.

Sure enough, the text wasn't long in coming.

You killed a mamushi? Do you still have the body?

No. I burned it.

Next time, call me.

Why?

What you do is, you skin it then cook it over the fire. It's delicious, particularly the tail. It goes really well with some saké.

I should've known. Food. Snacks. *Otsumami.* My father-in-law is an expert on things that go well with saké. After surviving the Battle of the Boulders, the last thing I wanted to do was skin, cook and eat the vanquished. It seemed disrespectful. It seemed barbaric. It seemed gross. I decided then and there to forswear the role of snake-battler and devote my shovel to peace. I invested in nets and grappling poles to humanely catch and relocate any legless intruders. Never again shall blood be spilt on my soil and no snake shall suffer the indignity of going well with my father-in-law's saké. My garden from that moment on became a place of peace and co-existence.

Well, apart from the centipedes. Those fuckers will rue the day.

Since then I've encountered three more *mamushi.* Two met their maker, one escaped. I hate it. I feel so bad every time but the risk is too high.

However, I haven't let my father-in-law anywhere near them. Each one has ended up in the compost or the fire. He found one in his own garden and proudly, almost sarcastically, produced it at a barbecue. I near upchucked.

My father-in-law is a Practical Man. An outdoorsman. He can take down a tree, skin a snake, catch a fish, build a house. Minori and I have one plan in the event of a huge earthquake/tsunami/zombie apocalypse: head straight to wherever Yoji is and wait it out. He'll know what to do. Probably already has everything organised: bags of rice stashed away, seeds, gallons of water and gasoline. He's not a survivalist in the right-wing nutbag in Montana kind of way, more just someone who doesn't trust anyone else and would much rather do it himself.

My father had an interesting relationship with his father-in-law. My dad is a city boy, a Glaswegian, but early on he left the city, wandered the world first as a hitch-hiker, then in the Merchant Navy where he was, by mutual agreement, considered the worst waiter ever to sail the high seas, before ending up in the North East of Scotland. My grandfather was another Practical Man. Fixed his own cars, built his own furniture. Why pay someone else to do it? When I was a child he had a sideline in buying old caravans, gutting them, doing them up and selling them. There were caravans everywhere, and many of our holidays were taken that way. My dad helped him in this, learning along the way, picking up both the skills and confidence to become a Practical Man himself, something he now excels at.

Me? Books and poetry and music and art and theatre. I can cook and I can tell you a lot about the history of Japan. I'm a Leftie, a liberal, a *Guardian* reader. I am, from a Practical Man's perspective, hardly a man at all. Moving to the countryside unlocked that and, under Yoji's tutelage, I've developed DIY and gardening skills I never thought possible. I have built, cut, painted, planted, burned and shaped. I have green fingers and calluses, I have chopped wood with an axe and harvested kilos of potatoes. I've come a long way, yet somehow I still don't feel like a Practical Man – not really. How long would I survive if disaster came? Could Minori and I ever be self-sufficient?

One of the main reasons we wanted to move into the countryside – apart from mild misanthropy and a penchant for the inconvenient – was to grow our own vegetables and move towards self-sufficiency. With the news full of North Korean missile tests and Trump's bellicose diplomacy in the region – only a small step beyond 'I know you are but what am I?' – and too many hours watching post-apocalyptic dramas, self-sufficiency has never seemed less like a lifestyle choice and more like getting a head start. I try to keep it more *The Good Life* than *The Year of the Flood*, but a fabulous short story I read online that I've never been able to find again (I think it was in Words Without Borders but it doesn't seem to be there any more) laid its groundsheet and pinned its guy ropes into my cerebellum. In it, a massive earthquake leaves Tokyo uninhabitable, and millions of Tokyoites, unable to survive without restaurants and convenience stores, descend on rural Japan. It soon turns into a battle between starving refugees and farmers without enough to share round.

My pitiful attempts to feed two people from the ground would hardly divert even the most peckish locust, but when you're weeding, pruning, digging and generally waging eternal war against entropy, you have a lot of time to let your mind off the leash to run a marathon through potential.

One of my successes though was shiitake mushrooms. You get a section of tree about a metre or so long and at least 20cm in diameter, drill holes in it and plug it with spores. Then you leave it in the garden, in a dark, wet spot where fungus is as fungus does. Mushrooms, like teenagers, vampires and Mrs Hasegawa, don't react well to sunlight. She keeps the typhoon screens over her windows closed at all times, so the house looks abandoned and whenever she ventures outside she does so covered head to toe in fabric, like a cross between the invisible man and a laundry pile. As a Scot, I don't understand this fear of the sun. Avoiding sunburn is one thing, but the terror of exposing even one skin cell to daylight is neurotic. My wife's friends are like that. When we visit them, regardless of the time of day and year, the curtains are closed and the a/c or heaters are on. When we invite them round for a barbecue, they insist on sitting inside while I cook by myself in the garden. Maybe they are really mushrooms in disguise.

So we got a bumper crop. Too much for us to handle. Some we dried and stored, some we gave to neighbours and family, but for a few days we ate shiitake with everything. My preference is to lightly fry them in chilli-infused olive oil with a dash of lemon, my wife prefers them fried with butter and salt. Mushrooms are like pancakes. We experimented with flavours, toppings, accompaniments. A particular success was serving them with a very spicy homemade salsa, dipping wedges like carrots in hummus or sausages in honey.

One evening, after Minori had gone to bed and I was up watching *The Walking Dead* and thinking about canned goods and whether I could dig a shelter in the garden, I spotted a couple of saucer-sized shiitake on the chopping board, left over from dinner prep. I quickly sliced them up, grabbed the salsa, a glass of red wine, and set to munching.

About two in the morning I wake up.

'Something's wrong.' I shake Minori awake.

'Ugh. What is it?'

'My mouth . . . my face feels strange. Like it's swelling.'

I grab for the light switch, a string hanging down with a luminescent knob on the end, missing it a couple of times as it dances like a firefly.

She examines me, prods my cheeks, touches my forehead. 'Is it just your face?'

'My whole body feels hot.'

'How much did you drink?'

'It's not that, I don't know what this is. I don't like it.'

'It sounds like an allergic reaction. What did you eat and drink tonight?'

'Everything. Same as you. Nothing unusual.'

She sits up, her back against the headboard and starts tapping at her phone. I go through a list of meat, vegetables, drinks. Nothing out of the ordinary. Nothing she didn't eat too.

'Do you need to go to hospital?'

'I don't know. If it gets worse, my tongue . . .'

She drives me to the nearest emergency hospital, about thirty minutes away. Inside the hospital a bored middle-aged man sits behind the reception desk. All the lights are off apart from the ones above the entrance, in his little cubbyhole, and along a single corridor straight ahead. The corridors to the left and right are pitch black. The only sound is the automatic door juddering open.

Minori explains what's happened while I hang back. He says nothing, hands over a clipboard. She takes the forms, hands them to me, and we retreat to the benches.

It's a standard medical questionnaire: conditions, allergies, medications. When we reach the 'allergies' box she hesitates.

'Only cats. But I haven't eaten any in ages.'

'You must be allergic to something. I think it might have been the mushrooms.'

'I ate them yesterday and I was fine. You can't develop an allergy overnight.'

'It must be them.'

I return the clipboard and pen. He points at the benches, never makes eye contact. I rejoin her, look over the posters and signs. Everything's aimed at the elderly – osteoporosis, dementia, flu shots. They know their demographic. Posters on sexual health or MMR vaccines would be wasted here. Japanese hospitals are divided, different departments scattered around the cities. An Ear, Nose and Throat clinic over here, Orthopaedics over there, Gynaecology in another location. In a country with a huge ageing population, the majority of emergencies – the things ambulances get called out for – involve the elderly. Heart attacks, strokes, dementia-related accidents. I don't just feel like a foreigner in here, I feel like a visitor from another time. The young (or relatively young) of Japan – natives and foreigners alike – are afterthoughts of policy, the remainder at the end of a calculation.

A door opens, casting light across the lino like something out of *The X-Files*. I go in.

Ten minutes later, I come back out.

'Well?'

'It was the shiitake.'

'Did you get a shot?'

'Yeah. We have to wait about half an hour to see if it works or if I have another reaction.'

'How come you're suddenly allergic to them?'

'I'm not. I ate a couple more after you went to bed. Raw.'

'Raw? So?'

'The doctor said that shiitake contain something called lentinan but that even lightly cooking them destroys it.'

'So if you eat them raw . . .'

'It's pretty rare. About one in five hundred people react. I'm special.'

'You're an idiot.'

'They were so delicious.'

'They taste even better cooked.'

'My way seemed easier.'

Japan is safe. Unless you are a snake in my garden or I serve you a mushroom.

Bugs

Japan is safe, yet my mother is reluctant to come and visit. In fourteen years she's been just the once. She had a grand old time. We took her to the famous places, she stocked up on the famous souvenirs, turned down the famous dishes (curried horse-meat donuts, what's not to like?), and survived the epic planes, trains and automobiles that indirectly connect small-town Japan with small-town Scotland. Yet she's reluctant to return.

It may have something to do with the previous chapter. My mother is not a fan of insects, of things that creep and things that crawl, things that buzz and things that bug. I can't say I blame her, but she takes the fear to the levels of an art form. She once jumped out of a moving car on a narrow cliff-edge road in the north of Tenerife because she heard something say 'buzz'.

The unwillingness to come began with the knowledge that there are cockroaches. In Scotland cockroaches are a rarity. Cockroaches like the heat. Scotland has eschewed heat. To get cockroaches in Scotland, there has to be something in your establishment that induces the roach to brave the climate. Dirt, usually. An inadherence to health and safety regulations. Or maybe it's the benefits, since that's supposedly the reason everyone else comes. Maybe they're after our jobs. Katie Hopkins says foreigners are cockroaches. The Japanese far right says Koreans are cockroaches. It's strange how the foreigner-hating members of any community seem to have so much in common with the foreigner-haters in other countries. They share concepts, linguistic tics, ideologies. It's almost as if people were all the same and geographic origin is somehow irrelevant. Anyway, I've gone off track. Cockroaches. Not the far right.

I know which I'd rather welcome into my home. At least cockroaches have the common decency to hide in the shadows, to secrete themselves inside walls rather than drive everyone else up them. In hot countries there are cockroaches. It's a fact of life. But they can be squashed. As can fascists.

She isn't a fan of snakes either. Nor centipedes. Her disinclination became inflamed following a description of a centipede I encountered lurking under a rock while I was building my fire pit. About a foot long and aggressive. I agree with her there. These bastards give me the creeps, the heebies and the jeebies. Scotland isn't over-endowed in the centipede department. We lack dangerous creatures in general. It's too cold and wet for most, and those that did enjoy the climate – bears, wolves, Jacobites – have all been hunted to extinction.

Take the common UK centipede. It grows to a maximum of 3cm in length and can, if heavily provoked, give a sting that is comparable with a pin prick. I left Scotland when I was twenty-five and can honestly say that in that quarter century I can't recall ever seeing a single one. In Japan, in my garden, in the last twelve months I've engaged in mortal combat with dozens. So far I remain undefeated. So far. The Japanese centipede is a vicious bastard. They grow up to 20cm in length and are highly aggressive. If one stings you, it hurts. Not just a little: a lot. It's excruciating. There's very little you can do about it but ride it out. A couple of paracetamol won't cut it. These things ache.

Preparedness is the key. Like the undead and Smashing Pumpkins circa 1995, they only come out at night. During the day they sleep under rocks and are dozy when roused. They like the heat, the damp, and have a fondness for coming into houses and hiding out in clothes and bedding. All over the house and garden I keep long metal barbecue tongs and cans of centipede spray, a chemical concoction that freezes them in a thoroughly convenient and satisfying way, giving you time to grab them, separate them into sections (you'll want straight-edged tongs for this) and crush them. In summer – when they are most active – never walk around the house without turning the lights on. Give everything a quick shake – away from you – before putting it on.

If you're doing any kind of gardening, roll things over before lifting them. Wear thick leather gloves, the kind hawkers use. Knights' gauntlets work too. Shake your shoes before putting them on. Surround the house with a noxious powder that disappears the first time it rains. Never relax. Never surrender. Here, there is but one commandment: thou shalt not suffer a centipede to live. In my garden, you do unto them what Edward I did unto William Wallace.

So Mum was already reluctant to come. It became an inferno of disinclination when I mentioned the bee. Not just any bee, a huge bee, a massive bee, a behemoth bee – Beezilla.

Japan does an interesting line in bees. One abomination is the 'giant sparrow bee' (*osuzumebachi*) or Asian giant hornet. With a body length of about 45mm and a predilection for the colour black (a huge problem in a country where the natural hair colour is firmly fixed at that end of the spectrum), their stings can – and do – kill. Around thirty to forty people die every year. In 2016, 115 runners were stung when a marathon in Gifu passed underneath a hornet nest. Eight were hospitalised.

So here's the thing. They like the colour black, as I said. As a result, they have a frankly inconsiderate habit of climbing inside black clothing if it's hanging out to dry in the late afternoon/early evening. We are usually incredibly vigilant about taking the washing in long before the gloaming but one day we were both held up at work and didn't get home until late. I took the washing inside, shaking it first, but apparently not vigorously enough. In the living room, as I folded a T-shirt, the sound of a dentist's drill erupted from somewhere in the laundry pile.

In the ensuing chaos we caught it in a net and splatted it with a shoe, but not before smashing two lightbulbs, a wine glass and a vase. God help the dentist next time I need a filling.

To an extent I understand my mum's hesitation about visiting, but humans can get used to anything. The first Japanese centipede I saw induced nausea and a very real shiver down my spine, an instinctive reaction from somewhere deep in genetic memory. The last time, I tutted and reached for the tongs. Fear of things that can hurt you is perfectly rational. That's why there's no scientific term ending in -phobia for the fear of serial killers. My garden is a bit bitey, but it could be worse. So far there haven't been any wild boar or bears. Barbecue tongs only work on wild boar that's been pre-butchered.

Hunger Strike

As I mentioned earlier, my father-in-law is partial to snakes, ideally skinned and flame-grilled. He is the outdoor type and a walking refutation of the vegetarian argument that 'you wouldn't eat it if you had to kill it yourself'. Japan in general has a far more adventurous attitude towards food. It's the only place I've been where an honest description of haggis is met with 'Sounds nice, where can I get some?'. The first time Minori visited Scotland she returned with canned haggis as a souvenir. Her cousin ate it cold and raw straight from the can and claims to have enjoyed it. Yoji takes this to extremes and has a black sense of humour about the subject, spending a good five minutes explaining to me the best way to fatten up my pet turtles before making them soup in their own shell. To be fair, I did something similar with my niece's pet rabbit when I told her we eat rabbits in a delicious stew. She just looked at me like I was mental, which is her reaction to most things I do or say.

Food can be a pain in Japan. All foreigners who live here know and loathe the hassle that can come with public eating. Every dish laid before you is accompanied by the question *Taberaremasu ka?* – Can you eat this? – and followed by the kind of surprise usually only seen on the faces of simpletons at magic shows when you announce that yes, you can indeed eat potato salad/fried chicken/salmon. It's well meaning but inspired by a moronic media that believes its only role is to support the idea of Japanese cultural uniqueness. Over the years, we've managed to train my in-laws to stop asking, so it was with some disappointment at a barbecue early that first summer that I heard Minori's uncle say *'Taberaremasu ka?'* as he laid a plate of something in front of me.

'Yes, of course,' I answered, slightly more tersely than I intended and without even looking at the plate. Really, we're back to this? I thought as I reached out with my chopsticks and took something that looked worryingly like bacon made from Play-Doh, kind of white and pink, but in shades of those colours not found in nature. Some kind of reconstituted fish, I assumed, putting it in my mouth. It was revolting. Gelatinous and fatty. I quickly swallowed it down followed by an entire glass of beer.

'You've had it before?' Uncle said.

'I don't think so. What is it?'

'Did you like it? I got it as a gift. I've never tried it before either. To be honest, it isn't that great, is it? I didn't think you'd want to eat it. I didn't think any foreigners ate it.'

'What is it?' I could feel it settling greasily somewhere near the top of my stomach. I was getting worried.

'Whale bacon.'

'Whale! But that's . . .'

'Yeah.'

'It's what?' My wife came over and prodded the meat. As I slipped quietly to the bathroom and less quietly disposed of the whale bacon, an argument started up about the ethics and politics of whale hunting. No one was in favour of whale hunting. Rather, the argument revolved around what to do with an unwanted gift. Chuck it out was my wife's position. Free food is free food, said the uncle. If someone gives you a gift you don't just toss it away. You try it first, then give it to the dog.

Honestly, I think the way to stop whale hunting is to let people try eating it. Few people I know in Japan have ever tried it. Most never even think about it. According to various reports, the meat ends up either taking up space in freezers, unsold, or it's 'donated' to elementary school canteens. As Uncle proved, it's nearly impossible to even give the stuff away. It's utterly disgusting. There is no economic argument for hunting since that requires both supply and demand. There is literally no demand. The only argument the government have for continuing to hunt whales is that it's tradition. But 'tradition' doesn't automatically mean something is good and can't be ditched.

An open but amused attitude to food runs in the family. Yoji's ability to look at anything and see how it could be turned into food has immense benefits. Deer and wild boar are plentiful in Japan but are uncommon in restaurants or in the supermarket. People suggest it's because the meat 'smells', something they ascribe to lamb as well. I happen to love venison and wild boar, and do a good line in stews. My father-in-law can hunt, kill and butcher, but has never learned to cook beyond the open fire. Together we make a good team. He kills it, I cook it. Everyone wins. Except the animal, obviously.

And me.

'My dad needs your help.'

'Doing what?'

'He didn't say. Do you have plans on Saturday?'

'Nothing much.'

'He wants you to go with him to the cabin. He says to wear old clothes, things you can throw out afterwards.'

'What does he want me to do? Is he finally putting a toilet in?'

'Maybe.'

'Sure, tell him I'll meet him there.'

Minori's grandfather was from the deep countryside, a tiny mountain community in Gifu. The family still own the land and what we misleadingly call 'the cabin' is a falling-down house, more a wooden bothy, once inhabitable but now little more than a glorified shed, and too damp to even use for storage. When I first heard about this cabin in the mountains I immediately thought of it as a writing retreat. I read way too much Kerouac as a kid, and *Desolation Angels* had a big impact on me. The idea of being alone, in nature, with nothing to do but write, think, drink gallons of cheap wine and drunkenly shout at the trees is like catnip to my clichéd romantic soul. It took half an hour on the property to convince me this was not a goer. In fact, it took about thirty seconds in the cabin with the centipedes that squat there. In *Zen and the Art of Motorcycle Maintenance*, Robert M. Pirsig says that 'the only Zen you find at the tops of mountain is the Zen you take there'. You may have to import your own Zen but the bitey things are there waiting for you.

Yoji takes care of the place, and there's a vague plan that when his brother – whale bacon uncle – retires, they'll do the place up properly. Installing a toilet is high on everyone's list, so at least we can use it for barbecues – the cabin, not the toilet. I pull into the dirt road that winds to the place and park behind Yoji's old-man truck. All Japanese men in the countryside, when they reach a certain age, are apparently required by law to buy a Suzuki Kei truck, a Dinky Toys pickup truck in a uniform white with a top speed of slightly less than that of decaying hydrogen. I have no idea why all these men suddenly need a flatbed that can comfortably hold two suitcases and not much else but I've had plenty of time to ponder the question while being stuck behind them on single-track roads.

Something is squealing. The path curves around a large pond to the cabin, hidden behind overgrown weeds and trees. The squealing intensifies as the road bends and straightens to reveal Yoji. He's drinking a can of coffee, standing next to a massive wild boar in a cage. The wild boar is squealing. I have a sinking feeling.

Japan's pests don't just live under rocks. Bears, monkeys and wild boars are the scourge of the countryside. As far as I'm aware there aren't many bears around my part of Gifu – too much development, dams and quarries encroaching their territory. Further north, there are persistent stories of bears appearing in town, of hikers encountering them after a sharp turn in the trail. The Japanese black bear can weigh up to 120kg, and it is thought there are about 10,000 of them in the country. The Ussuri brown bear can reach 500kg and is fucking terrifying. Fortunately (for me) they are restricted to Hokkaido and have, as yet, not learned to use the ferry or found the entrance to the tunnel that connects Hokkaido to Honshu. The Ussuri are worshipped by the

Ainu, Japan's indigenous people, and on a recent trip to Hokkaido one old Ainu man showed me a claw and a tooth. We're in *Revenant* territory here.

Needless to say, hunting bears is allowed to keep the population manageable, but it is ecologically viable hunting, not the uncontrolled, semi-automatic bloodfest America goes in for. Saying that, bear stew is available in the more rural eateries, and, one day, I will give it a go, mainly so I can manufacture the following exchange:

Waiter: How's the stew?

Me: The seasoning is really good.

Waiter: How about the meat?

Me: It's a bit grizzly.

As a child raised on the Asterix comics, wild boar is a favourite of mine. But they – and monkeys – are more of a problem for farmers. They come down in the night and raid the crops, necessitating tall mesh fences and electric fences around farmland. Again, a check is kept on the wild boar population, and trekking through the hills will quickly bring you upon a cage baited and lying in wait.

Yoji provides, I prepare: this was the symbiotic relationship that, until I rounded the corner at the cabin, I thought was working well. Now Yoji, it seemed, was broadening the scope of the relationship, redefining what was involved in preparation. I was to be blooded, literally, into the ways of butchering.

I won't go into the details. Much like the bear stew, it is grizzly. It has a bloody ending. I upchucked.

Would you eat meat if you had to kill the animal yourself?

Hmmm, yeah. Still not eating snake though.

A Cheery Wave
from Stranded Youngsters

So, what made a thirty-five-year-old Scot decide to anchor the rest of his natural life to half an acre in central Japan?

Exile.

Not in a medieval banished-from-the-kingdom-for-looking-the-wrong-way-at-a-princess-of-the-realm way, but metaphorically, practically, emotionally, the UK has made it quite clear it doesn't want me. At least, not while I'm married to a foreigner. For the UK government, marrying a foreigner is tantamount to a crime against the state. One that warrants exile.

It was never meant to be this way. Not that I have any idea how it *was* meant to be, but this was never even a synaptic spark when I was young. I never read manga or watched anime, I had little interest in samurai movies and beyond the basics of the Pacific War at school and the Haruki Murakami books I read at uni, Japan meant little to me. If I was ever going to travel and settle outside Scotland it would most likely be Europe, but realistically Ireland. With a name like Maloney, a love of James Joyce and a strong but manageable addiction to Guinness, Ireland was always on the cards. And I so nearly ended up there.

I graduated from Glasgow University in 2004 with an MPhil in Creative Writing and took up an offer from my father to stay with him while I finished the novel I'd been working on as part of the course. I went back to working in the same pub I'd worked in as an undergraduate, finished *Sometimes Sleep*, and sent it out to publishers and agents. And waited.

And waited.

What I'd failed to realise and what people were quick to point out was that my novel was shite. Not just rough, not just in need of a damn good editing; no, it was shite. So that was me all out of good ideas.

My father, quite reasonably, wondered when I'd be leaving and getting a proper job, something an MPhil in Creative Writing doesn't prepare you for much. There didn't seem to be many of those around, certainly none I could imagine myself doing. I wasn't even sure what an accounts manager did (I'm still a bit vague) but that's all that was on offer. A friend of mine who had spent a year studying in Oslo knew someone there putting together a rep company to tour Ireland performing Shakespeare in primary and secondary schools. Chris was thinking about signing up. Was I interested?

An actor? Sure, I could do that. Nine months of travelling, that tickled something in me, lit a spark.

At the same time, my father suggested teaching English abroad. I knew people who'd done that in Romania, in Italy and in China. They all came back positive about their experiences but I had that block that many have, caused by that inane epigram: 'Those who can, do, those who can't teach.' I wanted to write novels, not teach English. Stupidly, I felt going into teaching would be like admitting failure. But my father had a point – I could use teaching English as a foreign language as a way to fund travel. I did some searches online and filled in application forms for companies in Japan, South Korea, Thailand, others. I didn't have any TEFL qualifications so that ruled Europe out, and many other countries. Japan seemed pretty relaxed about qualifications so I applied to a few companies there, my apathy flowing like water into any available crack.

In the meantime, we went to Oslo.

I'd never been to Norway before, and we timed it well, arriving as the snow was thawing, three men in our early twenties (another friend had come along for the ride). We did some sightseeing, drank as much as we could afford (not much), and slept on a cold, hard floor in a friend of a friend's spare room. I did some writing as well, none of it any good. A clichéd story about a refugee hiding in an abandoned church and a string of haiku, all consigned to the flames.

The Shakespeare tour wasn't going to work. I took an instant dislike to the organiser, Anthony, and the thought of spending nine months in his company was unbearable. While I didn't doubt his passion for Shakespeare and his vision to bring *King Lear*, *Macbeth* and *Romeo and Juliet* to the young of Ireland, he seemed far too unreliable on the logistical side of things. I immediately saw long stretches without money, confusion about accommodation and bookings, arguments about travel and baggage. Chris felt the same. We enjoyed the holiday and flew back to Scotland.

I returned to an email from a Japanese company called Nova offering me a job interview in London. I still had no real desire to go to Japan or to teach, but I was fast running out of ideas and my father was fast running out of patience. Besides, the interview was on a Friday morning. I could go down on the Thursday, do the interview, then enjoy a long weekend in London with some friends. It was too good an excuse to pass up.

The secret to succeeding in an interview is to not want the job. I arrived at the offices off Oxford Street totally relaxed, sailed through the interview and was in the pub with my friends by lunchtime, my biggest concern being the ridiculous beer prices.

I got the job.

The rest goes pretty much as expected. I fell in love with Japan and fell in love with Minori. We spent a year living back in Edinburgh in 2007 but decided Japan was a better bet. The economy was about to be flushed down the toilet by the very people charged with its care, and after a summer temping at the SQA and working a zero-hour contract at Berlitz, I'd had enough of the job market. Minori is a nurse, and if she wanted to work in Scotland she'd have to go back and redo most of her qualifications. In Japan we could both find work easily. Done.

But we're both travellers. We both said at the time that the return to Japan was only temporary. We'd be back in Scotland one day, or maybe somewhere else. Committing the rest of my life to Minori and committing the rest of my life to Japan weren't the same thing. We spoke at length. We were on the same page.

Then, in 2010, Britain voted in a Tory government by accident. In July 2012 the Conservative-Liberal Democrat coalition changed the immigration rules for non-EU spouses of UK citizens. To qualify for a visa, the UK citizen (me) had to earn more than £18,500 a year in the form of a salary from one source. This job had to be permanent and the employee had to have been in the job for a minimum of a year to qualify. If these criteria were met, the spouse (Minori) would have to pay £3,500 for their visa. If the criteria couldn't be met, the UK citizen had to have a minimum of £60,000 in savings.

The criteria specifically ruled out freelance work. As a freelance writer and editor who earned over the £18,500 minimum, my income was deemed irrelevant. If I decided to proceed and secure a permanent job with a salary over £18,500 (far from easy with the government sending the economy into a second recession), I would have to have lived apart from Minori for a year.

By comparison, if the spouse was an EU citizen, they paid £65.

These rules were racist and elitist. They punished UK citizens for having the audacity to marry foreigners and were organised to allow only Russian oligarchs and Arab sheikhs to come and live in the country. The argument given was that in order to allow free movement from the EU, they had to clamp down on non-EU citizens. However, in the EU referendum the push wasn't to liberalise the discriminatory rules against non-EU citizens to bring them into line with EU citizens; every piece of rhetoric was aimed at making it just as difficult for those married to EU citizens to live with them in the UK. For UKIP et al this wasn't about regaining control, it was about excluding and punishing.

Effectively, my country said, 'You choose: your country or your wife.'

I chose my wife. From that day on I considered myself in exile from the UK.

I applied for indefinite leave to remain in Japan. I paid ¥8000 (about £75) and got it.

*

'You're going to live here until you die?'

'Yes.'

We bought a house with a large garden in the centre of Japan, fixing our stamps (Japanese people don't sign, everyone has a unique stamp) to the mortgage papers and collecting the keys in May 2016. The whole thing terrified me.

When I first came to Japan in 2005 it was on a twelve-month contract, and at the airport my mother put the anxiety into perspective: 'If you hate it, just get on a plane and come home.'

In twelve hours we can be on the other side of the world. Another twelve and we're back home. Journeys that once took years are done in the time it takes to watch a couple of films, eat a couple of meals and doze fitfully. 'You can always come home.' Not any more. Home is half an acre in Gifu Prefecture. I have embraced exile. I am home.

I Am Not Batman

Minori was rightly worried about local responsibilities. In Japan, a culture which traditionally places high regard on social harmony and unselfish behaviour under all circumstances except those involving roads, you are expected to take part in events and perform duties that benefit the community. As people have moved from the countryside to the cities, leaving behind ancestral land in pursuit of what the US Declaration of Independence euphemistically refers to as 'happiness' and the rest of us call 'money', the tradition has waned. Urban life is unsuited to communal cohesion. Cities only work when we all accept a certain level of blindness, when we choose not to feel the bag pushed into our ribs on the subway, or pretend to be unaware of the smell coming from the back of the bus, when we understand that access to a small patch of garden necessitates the compromise of heavy footsteps upstairs and a higher risk of break-ins. The city-dweller must choose not to register the sweaty press of humanity mere inches away. It would drive us all mad otherwise. Humans did not evolve to be comfortable in swarms. In the city, famously, you are never more than a few metres from another human. China Miéville took this to extremes in his brilliant book *The City & the City*, imagining two cities superimposed one on the other, where 'noticing' the other city is a crime, an act of rebellion that could bring society to its knees.

In the countryside, noticing is a pastime. It's a vocation. It's raised to the status of an Olympic sport. Everyone notices everything. And this isn't suburban curtain-twitching, trying to get a peek at what number 22 is up to. I've become used to elderly men suddenly appearing in my garden, asking where I'm from and then criticising the way I'm digging/pruning/cutting. The postie has a new question about Scotland with every package. And a day never goes by without Asai passing comment on something he's seen over the hedge. 'Is your foot okay? You seem to be limping?' 'How's your wife? I knew you were away so I kept an eye on her.' 'Put on some weight, haven't you?'

He's well meaning, as most retired people with nothing to fill their days are, and it doesn't bother me much. I grew up in the countryside, and the oxymoronic urban invisibility gets to me, makes me feel lonely and isolated. One reason I wanted to move to the country was a latent hope for some kind of community spirit, a place where, at the very least, you could be on 'morning' terms with the neighbours. Minori disagrees. She finds it irritating, intrusive, to the point of paranoia. To her, Asai's well-intended eye is a big brother, a patriarchal gaze of elderly male Japanese presumption that she has always rebelled against. Her mother said, on our wedding day in Japan, 'Thank God you married her – she'd never have put up with a Japanese man. We all just assumed she'd never marry.' A sentiment, in reverse, of which a few of my friends and family informed Minori at our 'second wedding' in Scotland. There's someone for everyone, as they say.

For Minori, moving to a community with an onerous package of duties was out of the question. She doesn't want to be part of a collective, a cog in the wheel. When we moved in, the previous owner had built a fire pit in a nice spot quite near Asai's house. They were the same age, old friends, chatted all day. Minori refused to join me when I lit the fire. She felt we were being watched by our neighbours the whole time. So I rebuilt the fire pit further away. She finds it hard to relax under the gaze of others. I mind less. I bought this place so I had somewhere to relax, and as a foreigner in Japan I have had to get used to a certain amount of curiosity and scrutiny. Besides, me sitting by a fire with a beer and a book is hardly the kind of viewing that is going to get Netflix beating down my door for the rights.

'It's all right for you, it's me that'll end up doing everything. You'll pretend you don't understand and I'll be stuck with all the old grannies.'

She had a point. It's a cowardly thing, but it's every immigrant's trump card, the ace hidden behind the mandatory identity card, literally a get-out-of-jail-free card. The shrug, the embarrassed smile, 'I'm sorry, officer, I no understand.'

The one-size-fits-all approach to community service doesn't just affect incomers or those with small families. In our second year in the village, it was Hasegawa's turn to be *hanchō*, a twelve-month position that involves things like attending meetings of all the area's *hanchō* and going door to door collecting annual dues. For a woman in her seventies who banned herself from driving after an accident a few years ago, this is nigh on impossible. She relied for the whole year on favours from the other neighbours, driving her around, performing her tasks. It would've been a lot easier just to excuse her, but no, this is how things are done. Every household must take its turn.

This is why Minori very carefully researched the expectations of the area before we moved in. Four clean-up days a year, a New Year meeting, and with twenty households in the group, your turn at being *hanchō* comes once a generation. When we moved in, we made a deal. When it was our turn to be *hanchō*, Minori would do it. The need to read and write Japanese to a native level effectively ruled me out. In return, I'd do the other duties. On paper, a fair idea, but that didn't stop me trying to wriggle out of it when the first clean-up day came round.

My first experience was the litter collection. Split into teams, the theory is that we cover a certain area picking up rubbish – man-made or acts of God – thereby bringing beauty and order to our pocket of Japan. In theory. As any economist, political leader or parent will tell you, the gap between theory and practice is big enough to handbrake-turn a double-decker bus through.

Litter collection is designated a man's job. Some jobs here are women's jobs, like cleaning the meeting hall, guarding the aforementioned garbage sites (and cleaning them afterwards), and serving snacks and drinks at the meetings. Anything outdoors is a man's job. We prune trees, trim the verges with unnecessarily powerful but fun strimmers, massacre bamboo groves with Home Centre-approved serrated machetes, and walk the streets keeping it safe from stray tissues and cigarette butts. I haven't seen this demarcation specified in writing, but it is *understood*. It was, therefore, with much amusement that my wife waved me off at seven in the morning, barely raising her head from the pillow to laugh.

Our team consists of me, Asai, Goto-san, a divorced man in his fifties who lives alone, and Ishikawa, who has three happy, highly energetic, noisy young daughters and leaves for work early, returning late. I am meeting Goto for the first time. Ishikawa grunts an *ohayo* before releasing a smoker's cough that sounds like an IED going off under a tank. Goto gives me a nod and the last two syllables of an *onegaishimasu*. It's Sunday morning, we all work hard, none of us want to be doing this and, by the look of things, I'm not the only one who indulged in a little light refreshment the night before.

Prepped in advance by Asai, I have a pair of gloves and a plastic bag. Goto has a bag sticking out of his pocket and no gloves. Asai has a pair of gloves tucked under his belt and no bag. Ishikawa has a can of coffee and a packet of Mild Sevens. We set off down the street.

The thing is, our area is spotless. The only people who ever come here are residents, family, or those on business, delivering, fixing or selling things. There's no through road. No one litters. Anything the wind brings in from outside is immediately picked up. There are no businesses that might inadvertently cause trash (there are literally no businesses; a local ordinance stipulates that the land here can be used for residential or farmland, nothing commercial). So this is a waste of time.

We walk about fifty metres down the road. I find a PET bottle cap that seems to have been embedded in the ground since the Palaeocene and prise it out. We continue. Asai fills the silence by pointing out which vegetables are growing in each patch. Each patch is the same as the one before. We pass another team with similarly sullen *ohayo*-s. Are they in our area or are we in theirs? They have empty bags as well. Asai leads us through a short cut by the meeting hall and loops us back home. Ishikawa drops his cigarette end in his can and drops the can in the bag. We reach home. Asai goes inside and comes out with four cans of coffee. We sit on his wall drinking them, him talking about the weather and the trees, us three silent but for slurps and sighs. Goto gives us another -*masu* and disappears inside. It's 7.17 a.m.

'Is that it?' I ask Asai.

'We were seen,' he says. 'It's enough.'

The reality of things rarely matches our trepidation. All the roles and duties that come with joining a small community in Japan can be intimidating. I'd been dreading having to take my place as a fine, upstanding pillar of society. As it turns out, everyone else dreads it too. Duties are meant to be onerous, otherwise we would call them something else. To fit in, all it takes is some effort, and to be seen to be making an effort. By 7.30 that Sunday morning I was out weeding and watering, just like everyone else in the village. Apart from Ishikawa. He sat for a while on Asai's wall, listening to the Sunday morning chaos echoing from his living room, enjoying a moment of solitude.

The Hissing of Summer Lawns

When I was twelve my parents separated and my father moved out. He remained nearby, and we had regular contact with him, but it was tough for all concerned. My mother is a nurse, with all the night shifts and irregular working hours that come with that underappreciated job. Seriously, as I write this Alexis Sanchez has made twelve appearances this season (2018–19) for Manchester United, seven of which came from the bench, out of a potential thirty-three at this stage in the season. He is a striker, so scoring goals is pretty much his job description. He has scored one goal. He is paid £300,000 a week plus bonuses, effectively to train and show up on match day. The average salary for an NHS nurse in the UK is £25,820 a year.

This, right here, is my problem with capitalism and the society it has created. The market decides value, and a man who keeps himself fit and very, very occasionally scores a goal is considered sixty times more valuable to society than someone whose job description includes stopping you from dying. That is capitalism. That is the free market. I have nothing against Alexis Sanchez – I'm sure if someone offered me £15 million plus a year I'd take it – but anyone who looks at that pay differential and says the foundations of our society are not fucked up is either an idiot or a psychopath (the two groups of people capitalism seems to reward).

Anyway, with our family situation changed I had to take on a larger share of household tasks, from cooking and cleaning to garden maintenance. Onerous as it was at the time it stood me in good stead for the future. (As an adolescent boy I had more pressing calls on my schedule than making big pots of chilli con carne for the freezer or ironing – I still hate ironing, and apart from my shirts for work, never iron anything. Who needs it? It's a hangover from those British days when you were so worried about what your neighbours would think of you that you'd iron your bed sheets. Who irons bed sheets? No one sees them apart from you and the people you invite in there and, trust me, no one has ever got to the threshold of the bedroom, lipstick smeared, clothes already undone, and gone, 'Wait, are those creases in the sheets? I'm sorry but I'm out of here.'). Every child, boy and girl, should be taught how to look after themselves. That, at least, is one useful thing parents can do. If you are sending your son off to university unable to work a washing machine, you've failed somewhere along the way.

When I left home most of those skills came in handy but the ability to run a Flymo over the lawn was a club that I never needed to take out the bag. From going off to university in Aberdeen until moving to rural Japan, I lived in apartments, and landlords and fellow tenants tend to frown on people who try to mow the balcony. However, it was a club in the bag nonetheless, so at least one aspect of land maintenance could be taken for granted.

Words I didn't know in Japanese before the first time I had to cut the grass:

Lawnmower
Strimmer
Two-stroke engine
Two-stroke engine oil
Rotating blade
Rotating plastic wire
Allen key
Visor
Bloody welts

Yoji presented me with an old strimmer he'd picked up somewhere and set about teaching me how to use and maintain it. In *Zen and the Art of Motorcycle Maintenance*, Pirsig posits two types of motorcyclist, each of which is meant to stand as a proxy for humanity in general. There are those like the narrator's friend, John, who buys a powerful and expensive BMW motorbike and refuses to learn the first thing about how it works. Consequently, whenever something goes wrong he has to take it to the shop and pay for someone else to fix it. The narrator himself, despairing of his friend's stubbornness, believes in a more symbiotic relationship between man and machine. He fixes one problem on his Honda with a piece fashioned from an aluminium drinks can. He gets his fingers in there, his hands dirty. As a result, he argues, he is freer. John is forever reliant on experts, many of whom aren't, and is often ripped off. The narrator can fix things on the fly, has a much deeper understanding of his machine, and as a result is reliant on no one. John is the modern world: shiny, convenient, enslaved. The narrator is a purer form of humanity: dirty, rough around the edges, hard-working but free. I adore this book, and it's an important bonding point with my father and me, but I can never read that passage without hanging my head. As much as I would love to think of myself as the narrator – free, self-reliant, in touch with the deeper things of the world – I am much more like John. Machines make my head numb. Engineering, cogs and gears, currents and switches are, to me, like the plot of *Sex and the City*: I'm told it makes sense but I can't see it myself.

I am like John. Yoji is like the narrator. Plus, I don't know any of the vocabulary. You know that Gary Larson cartoon: 'What we say to dogs/ What they hear'? The lesson goes something like that, but with prepositions and verbs rather than the dog's name.

'Blah blah blah into blah blah blah fasten to blah blah blah tighten. Blah blah blah carefully blah blah blah open. Blah blah blah cars and windows. Blah blah blah blah blah blah blah blah blah blah blah blah. Got it?'

'*Wakarimashita.*'

I fill her up, get her engine running. I'm aware that Yoji's stern eye is there for the benefit of his machine, not me. Tentatively I lower the blade into the midst of the grass. Instantly a little stone flips up and slams into my chest.

'Ow.'

'Yep. It hurts.' Yoji sits on the bench beside Minori and I get to work.

I took for granted that cutting the grass is cutting the grass. Flymo over lawn. Rake. Done. There are a number of problems with that. My garden doesn't have a lawn. This isn't really grass, not as a Brit would understand it. It's weeds, dandelions, crab grass, God knows what. Little leaves of something that Asai told me is as good as tempura – like Stalin through a Moscow creative writing class, my strimmer slices through them all. I'm getting the hang of this. I look up. Yoji and Minori have gone. I check my phone. I've been at it for forty minutes and I've covered about 3 per cent of my land.

Asai sticks his head over the wall. 'Hard work, isn't it?'

'Yeah.'

'The last owner always used to complain. By the time you get from one end to the other, you have to go back and start again.'

I doubt Asai has heard of the Forth Rail Bridge but that's what he's getting at. Things grow fast here in the heat of the summer.

'Is that why Zen gardens are covered in stone?'

'Could be.'

It takes me three and a half hours. Doing the edges by the road means I have to stop every time a car passes, lest a stone spin off into a windscreen. It appears the neighbours have all waited for this moment to go for a drive or cycle around like extras in a low-budget film shoot.

As I cut the engine Yoji reappears. 'How's your skin?'

I lift my T-shirt. My neck, chest and stomach are peppered with angry red welts. My thighs are the same. I look like a pepperoni pizza, a teenager's face, like an Anti-Vaxxer hit by a karma. It was never like this in Scotland. Is there anything in my garden that isn't out to get me?

It takes nearly half an hour for the vibrations in my arms to subside.

'How often do you think I'll have to do this?'

'Not too often. Every three weeks or so,' says Yoji.

'Every three weeks!'

'You'll get faster. You don't have to get every blade – no one's going to be playing tennis on it.'

'It's not the time.' It is partly. 'It's the pain.'

'*Shoganai*.' *C'est la vie*. There's no other way. Tough shit.

'Finished?' Asai calls over.

'For now.'

'It never ends. The last guy always said that.'

'Seems he was right.'

'Do you have fireflies in Scotland?'

The thing about older people is the non sequiturs. It's like a hobby, or a disease.

'Fireflies? I don't think so. I've never seen any.'

'Coming?'

I look at Yoji, lost. The two old men start talking in their fast, mumbled approximation of textbook Japanese and I'm more lost than Trump watching an episode of *The West Wing*.

'See if Minori wants to come.'

'What? Where?'

'Fireflies.'

I consider making a joke about Joss Whedon's series *Firefly* having been cancelled but I'm not old enough for anything that appears like a non sequitur. I can't imagine either of them being fans.

'I'll get her . . . Minori, they're going on about fireflies.'

'What about them?'

'I don't know, I got lost in the syllable soup.'

It soon becomes clear that there is a prime firefly viewing spot about ten minutes' drive away and Asai is taking us all in his SUV. As night falls we pile in, along with the whole Asai clan, ten of us in all, the kids squashed up together. I try to engage the kids in conversation, my Japanese being much closer to their level than the adults, but they're having none of it. The eldest is shy, the younger two uninterested. Yoji and Asai chat. Minori and Asai's wife, Junko, chat. Kensuke and his wife, Nozomi, chat. I slip into my default mode of half listening, half staring out the window.

It's the last day of firefly viewing, as the rainy season is coming the next day. We crest the mountain and turn down a side road that quickly becomes a dirt track and then disappears completely. We pile out into the twitching darkness. The kids run off up a narrow path to our right, and are soon lost in the black, their shouts echoing off the trees. Giant ruler-straight pines with gnarled, exposed roots, rustling pine needles, the crunch of our footsteps and maybe, just maybe, the snuffling of something on four legs all put me in mind of an ancient forest in a Ghibli film or, more worryingly for my sanity, *Twin Peaks*.

The path twists through the trees, brushing a stream briefly before climbing up and around a chain fence surrounding a reservoir. Branches hang low into the black water and the smell of decay, rotting vegetation in the summer humidity, hums in the air. We pass round the back of an old shrine, its sharp edges cutting against the fractal geometry of the forest. The sound of running water becomes clearer until suddenly the trees part and there before us is a ballet of stars, pale green lanterns flicking through the black canopy, coming together and breaking apart, the place transformed fully into a Ghibli paradise. Even the kids are hushed by the beauty of it, nature showing off to itself, the pure perfection of evolution on display.

Nuclear Holiday

Summer is usually the time for travel, but that first year in the village I wanted to spend as much time as I could at home. In August I'd be returning to Scotland for the Edinburgh International Book Festival so the rest of the time I devoted to immersing myself in the garden, getting a sense of the swirling winds and shifting sunlight. How much heat and light did each corner get? Where would be a good spot for a herb garden? Which trees were going to be a nuisance in a few years?

In fourteen years I haven't got used to the Japanese climate. I first came to Japan in the summer of 2005, and strolling out of Kansai Airport into a wall of humidity gave me the first of many 'we aren't in Kansas any more' moments. Although Kansas may have prepared me better than the North East of Scotland. Perhaps 'We're nae in Aiberdeen ony mair, Toto' is more apt. That summer I hid in air-conditioned rooms, refused clothes in all but the most necessary of circumstances and, once, spent two hours sitting in an ice bath, reading.

Things haven't improved. I haven't done a DNA test but I'd wager that every A, C, T and G in my body originated somewhere north of the 60th parallel. I once sweated so much in the Cambodian heat that despite its being in a supposedly waterproof case I had to dry my passport on the top of an Angkor Wat temple. My far more Southern European friend and the local tuk-tuk driver thought my impending dehydration hilarious.

Regardless of my internal thermostat's issues with the climate, moving out to the Japanese countryside and attempting self-sufficiency meant I paid attention to the weather cycles a lot more, something I'd neglected on ideological grounds. Quite simply, I can't stand people who think that the weather is a suitable topic of conversation. Don't get me wrong, the science of meteorology is fascinating – particularly the mathematics of fluid dynamics and chaos theory, and their application in mapping – but conversations about the weather that is literally happening in front, above and around us *at that exact moment* are absurd to me. This personal irritation is unfortunate, as I moved from Scotland to Japan – two countries bound together by an obsession with discussing the bleeding obvious in the blandest possible terms. Statements like '*samui ne*' (cold, isn't it?) and '*atsui ne*' (hot, isn't it?) are the conversational equivalent of mosquitoes – annoying, everywhere and impervious to swatting. Example: every August my mother says, 'We haven't had much of a summer this year.' She's said that every year since 1983. She probably said it in 1980, 1981 and 1982 as well but I have no coherent memories of that period. In the North East of Scotland, it isn't clear what she expects 'much of a summer' to be, but it can't realistically be anything other than the usual three days of sunshine in a row followed by a Noah-esque deluge.

Now, however, the vagaries of temperature and rainfall are part of my life. I watch temperatures the way models watch calories. I stare at the sky the way voyeurs stare at curtains. I check weather apps the way Trump checks his Twitter feed. Gardening and farming have introduced me to the unique experience of praying for rain.

I'm from Scotland. We all know the stereotype: it rains. People comment on the rain in Scotland as if the natives are: a) unaware of it; and b) can do something about it. Scotland is part of an island, west of which is the Atlantic Ocean – of course it rains. It would be weird if it didn't. It's strange how other countries, England specifically, use something over which we have no control as a way of having a go at us, but there you are. Rain isn't a big deal. You open the curtains, see that it's raining, shrug, and get on with your day. There's no such thing as bad weather, just bad clothes. Unless you're planning a barbecue on a nudist beach, I guess.

Japan is supposed to have a specific rainy season which apparently runs from mid-June to mid-July, though climate change is messing with this schedule. The oft told joke that the Japanese weather forecast is printed in the back of the phonebook is no longer funny-because-it's-true (if it ever was funny – and besides, when was the last time you saw an actual phonebook?). Still, you can count on one surefire thing: summer in Japan is *atsui* as fuck.

Apart from a few overnighters in the mountains, I spent July hosting barbecues, sorting out my garage, chopping and pruning and digging. I expected to feel the guilt of not using all those long summer weeks off work to explore the world, see new countries and drink exotic beers. I've long loved travel but I never embraced it fully when I was at university and had the time, if not the money. I was a secret introvert, with a fear of confrontation and a huge dollop of social awkwardness hidden behind bluster and pints. It made me somewhat small C conservative in my choices and it was only coming to Japan that changed me, an event so wholly out of character it effectively remade me from the inside out.

Since then I've tried to catch up. Every chance I get, a new prefecture or a new country. If I haven't hit at least a handful of new destinations each year, then it's been a wasted year. I tend to alternate between domestic and international summers, and that year was supposed to be an international one, but my garden called louder. I must be getting older. I used to view home as somewhere you kept your stuff in between adventures; now it's somewhere to be when you aren't forced to go elsewhere. You can't get into trouble at home, or at least the opportunities are much rarer. Getting into trouble while travelling? That's a doddle.

With the exception of Okinawa, Japan doesn't really exist in the popular imagination as a beachy kind of place. Temples and castles, neon and nightlife, that's what you come to Japan for. And to be fair, most of the beaches aren't worth the name. Heavy industrialisation, light pollution regulations and a population that fears direct sunlight the way many Scots fear the vegetable (a stereotype embarrassingly all too true – I have encountered Scots in every corner of the world clinging desperately to the idea that anything green is irredeemably yucky). However, there are some great spots, particularly along the northern Sea of Japan coastline. The beach at Kanazawa is gorgeous and kitted out with the kind of open-air bars that are rare in Japan and which make it all too easy to fall asleep with your skin dangerously under-creamed.

My first encounter with a Japanese beach was at Tsuruga in Fukui. It's quite Scottish in appearance, backed by pine trees, flat and curved around the bay. It reminds me a bit of the beach at Loch Morlich, near Aviemore. I'd returned a few times since that first trip, and felt like I knew the place reasonably well, so when a friend, Robert, was out visiting one summer five or so years ago, we decided to go wild camping along the coast and Tsuruga seemed the ideal starting point. It was really hot, and the idea was to take a couple of days and walk around the peninsula that sticks out into the sea to the east of Tsuruga, just sleeping on the beaches. Despite it being the height of August, there was always the chance of a squall or storm, so the sky couldn't be trusted not to fall on our heads. We didn't have a tent, but I did have a big blue tarpaulin. I took that, plus some rope, and figured we could make a shelter if it rained. It seems to work for homeless people in the parks of Nagoya, so it would be good enough for us. We got the bus to Tsuruga and when we arrived, it was torrential. It was about nine in the morning and we walked all day, until about 3.30, when the rain finally stopped and we decided it was time to find a spot to camp. We'd been walking along the side of the road all day and as we got farther and farther from Tsuruga the amount of traffic decreased except for cement trucks. There were hundreds of them going in each direction. Nothing else on the road, just these cement trucks. As we walked we speculated where they were going and coming from. Building a new highway? Some factories? We couldn't work it out and there was nothing on my map. Just as we were thinking about stopping, a police car came screaming up beside us, lights and sirens going, and these two cops jumped out. Proper country-side cops, old, grumpy, no English.

*

So we pull the stupid foreigner routine. Basic Japanese, keep going back to the dictionary. They ask for our ID, ask a bunch of questions, where we work, that kind of thing. Then they ask where we're going. I show them on the map. We're going around this peninsula, camping.

'No,' says Grumpy Cop senior, 'you're not.'

'Why not?'

'No campsites.'

Now, as far as I know wild camping isn't technically illegal in Japan but I figure they're not going to be happy with the idea of us sleeping rough, so I just shrug. 'So we can't go on?'

'No, you have to go back.'

'But it's half-past three. It took us about six hours to get here. Is there a bus?'

'No.'

'A train?'

'No.'

'So what should we do?'

They talk to each other then decide. 'Get in the car.'

'Are you arresting us?'

'No. We'll drive you back.'

We've got no choice really and I'm not going to argue with two cops. So we get in the back of their tiny cop car. Us, two big foreigners, each with a backpack, and all their cop gear. The car's so full and so heavy we can barely get up the hill. By this point we've decided this is hilarious and keep trying not to laugh. The cops are in the front discussing us in Japanese, thinking we can't understand them, calling us idiots. One refuses to believe that I work at a university, that someone clearly so idiotic could have a decent job like that. I'm translating what they're saying for Robert, who is also trying not to laugh. They drive us to the top of a hill and stop, tell us to get out. There's nothing there, just the road tipping down the other side and overgrown brush in every other direction.

'What do we do?'

'At the bottom of this hill there's a campsite. It's closed but next to it is a police station. You can stay in the campsite tonight. They are waiting for you. Tomorrow you go home.'

'Okay.'

We get out, thanking them. They watch us walk off. Once we are clearly doing what they want, the car heads back the way it came. Obviously this hill marked the end of their patch, so we were now someone else's problem. We turn and watch them go.

'What do you think that was all about?'

'No idea.'

'Thank God they didn't ask to see our tent.'

The rain started again and the blue tarpaulin proved worse than useless that night. Soaked, exhausted and now failing to find it all quite so funny, we packed up at first light, found a bus to Tsuruga and took the cops' advice, headed straight for home.

Once there, Minori did a bit of hunting online. 'That explains it.'

'What?'

'That peninsula has four nuclear reactors. Two foreigners with backpacks walking towards four nuclear reactors. One of those truck drivers called the police.'

'Why?'

'They must have thought you were terrorists.'

August in Japan can get so hot and dry that farmers tend to leave things fallow. A few herbs grow, and with shade and water you can coax some life out of peppers and peas, but unless you want soaring water bills, it's better just to wait it out. The planting season begins again in September, when the temperature starts to drop. In the meantime, I watched YouTube videos, read books, cross-referenced English information with Japanese websites, got a planting and harvesting calendar from the Home Centre and turned my attention to the house.

It hadn't been our primary reason for moving here but since the vagaries of the climate meant we had to spend much time inside comforted by the air conditioners or heaters, we had to make the place at least habitable. The previous owners had seemingly got a job lot of wallpaper from the laziest designer ever, and every room bar one – floors, walls and ceilings – was covered with off-white, grass-pattern embossed paper. I hate having workmen in the house. I'd rather do all the work myself, and the Ice Age it's going to take for me to get that done means I can take my time and get a feel for each room, learn its personality and decorate accordingly.

Since August is too hot to be outside, I decide to tackle the *tatami* room. The biggest room in the house, the previous owners used it in the traditional way. When we viewed the house it was a cold, dark, depressing place. There was a family shrine, a few hanging scrolls of the wispy-Chinese-mountain style and cupboards full of wallpaper offcuts.

The shrine departed with them, and the scrolls and wallpaper were left as gifts, or annoyances. I decided the room would be much better suited to my guitars and related appliances, a projector and screen, a big-ass stereo system (to use the jargon of audiophiles) and two of those chairs Chandler and Joey refused to leave in *Friends* (though not the electric one they should have made Ross sit in).

I stripped the paper from the *shoji* (paper and wood doors), leaving the beautiful maple frames. I took the thick curtains off the window to allow in light for the first time in possibly decades. That helped a little but the main problem was the walls. To offset the warm, light wood, the previous owners had painted them what I can only describe as *Exorcist* green. I looked at the walls much like Brits are looking at the current government, thinking, This has got to go.

The walls required a specific kind of paint for what they call 'sand walls', which, much like imagery, I had to layer on with a trowel. This posed no significant problems on the big open expanses of wall, but the pure, pristine maple wood edges right up against the hideous green were a challenge. Even with enough tape and plastic sheeting to make the room look like a set from *American Psycho,* trowelling thick paint without going over the lines was tricky. I wished I'd paid more attention at school when we did painting by numbers instead of committing the laws of osmosis and diffusion to memory. Although at least the latter did remind me to open the windows before I got wasted on the fumes.

All together, with drying time and second coats, it took three days. There were a few wayward dabs on the wood but they came right off with a wet cloth. The walls were now a dramatic bright white, like teeth in a toothpaste advert, clothes in a washing powder advert, or hosts on *Fox News*. Unfortunately, the *tatami* had been defiled, streaked with paint like someone had moved Harvey Weinstein's favourite pot plant. I didn't mind too much though, as it technically helped in the ongoing debate over whether to leave the *tatami* or replace it with floorboards.

At the end of the third day Minori came home from work and I met her at the door like an excited Alsatian, flushed with energy at having finished the job myself and having had a beer or two in celebration to release the accumulated tension of three days listening to Dinosaur Jr and The Replacements. I should know by now that the moments after returning from work aren't my wife's best. She hasn't learned that shouting at bad drivers on the commute gets it out of your system before crossing the domestic threshold, a trick my fellow commuters are aware I long ago mastered. I should know this about her, but like Bill Murray in *Groundhog Day*, or Melania Trump, I foolishly assume each day might be different.

'Come and see what I did.'

'Hang on. Let me sit down for a minute.'

'You've just been sitting in the car.'

'Okay. Show me.'

'Taa-daa!'

She walks around the room much like the drill sergeant inspecting the troops in *Full Metal Jacket*.

'It's good.'

'Thanks.'

'Especially over here. You can see how much you improved.'

'What do you mean?'

'Well, I can tell that you started in that corner and finished here. It looks professional here.'

And a man claims to have invented negging.

There are few things as pathetic as an enthusiastic male ego punctured by the well-placed lance of indifference. I spent the rest of the evening in a sulk, caught between childishly wanting to destroy my work in a fit of pique and avoiding facing up to a summit of achievement that turned out to be false. I'd taken down the tape and sheets but she was right. The earliest parts looked patchy and flaky, like a Trump appointee's grasp of climate science, and needed attention. But I couldn't find the energy. If you don't stand too close, you can't see the corners of green, the chips of paint.

In August I packed my bags and set off alone for Scotland. While I was away I entrusted Minori with the care of our two pet turtles, Lisa and Lincoln. For the moment they were living in a large plastic box I'd filled with rocks, plants and other things turtles like, such as pizza. When we bought them they were coin-sized but had since grown to something like a Digestive biscuit. The plan was to build a series of ponds around a gazebo and give one of them over to the turtles. In the meantime, they seemed happy enough with their box.

After ten days soaking up every experience of Edinburgh during the festival – surely one of the most magical places in the world – I came back to a sheepish wife.

'What's happened?'

'Lisa died.'

'Did you feed them?'

'I did. Exactly as you told me.'

'So what happened?'

'I don't know. Lisa wouldn't eat. Then I realised she hadn't moved for a few days so I poked her and she still didn't move. I got her out of the water and she still didn't move. So I put her in the freezer.'

'You . . . what?'

'I put her in a zip-lock bag in the freezer.'

'Why?'

'So you could see her. I didn't know if you'd believe me.'

'What? Why wouldn't I believe you?'

'I don't know. It just seemed the right thing to do.'

'She's in the freezer? With the food?'

'In a zip-lock bag. Do you want to bury her?'

'Um. Yeah. We'd better before your dad tries to cook her.'

The first thing I planted in my garden, as the summer ended and things came back to life, was my pet turtle, in amongst the roots of a cherry tree. Cherry blossom is the Japanese symbol of life and death, its beauty fierce but short, there for a moment and then forever gone.

Idiot Wind

Typhoons, like earthquakes, are not something the average Scot has much experience of. Cold, we know. Rain, absolutely. No bother there. Wind? You ever walked up King Street in Aberdeen? Boeing could test engines there. If you leave your parka unzipped, you can paraglide from the Lemon Tree to the Bobbin. Njord, Fūjin, Aeolus, Venti, Borrum, Amun and Oonawieh Unggi (look them up. I did. I thought Venti was the god of big coffee and Aeolus the god of nipples) could have a G7 (Seven Gods) summit outside the bus depot and the first item on the agenda would be to move somewhere less breezy. But the closest Scotland ever got to a typhoon – bearing in mind typhoons, hurricanes and cyclones are the same thing, just starting in different parts of the world – is Hurricane Bawbag.

Best. Name. Ever.

For those unfamiliar with Scotland's gift to meteorological history, a small recap. Hurricane Bawbag began life as the extratropical Cyclone Freidhelm (I know, right? Even Blowy McBlowface would've been better), which made landfall on 8 December 2011. It caused the usual damage and inconvenience, leading to it being labelled 'bawbag' – literally ball bag or scrotum, secondarily an annoying or irritating person.

By actual hurricane standards, it wasn't. It was, as the LED sign on the Forth Road Bridge famously announced, blowy as fuck, man.

I've long been a lover of extreme weather: waves, snow, lightning. If it scared the crap out of our ancestors so badly they invented gods to explain what the absolute fuck was going on with the world, it's all right in my book. Unfortunately, Gifu tends to be quite placid. We get snow, but nothing like Hokkaido. We get heat, but nothing like the South.

Typhoons tend to go around us, as if we smell bad and are best avoided. They swing north across the Sea of Japan or south by Nagoya. We get standard rain pushed in front of the storm but none of the actual storm itself. For more than a decade typhoons had been bouncing off Kyushu and Shikoku, the sky had been falling on everyone's heads but ours.

When the gods seek to punish us, they grant our wishes.

Predicting the path of typhoons isn't an exact science. There are so many variables that it would take Deep Thought more millennia to come up with an answer like 'northeast-ish' than it took him to hit on forty-two. But this one was easy. It was on a heading of nor-nor-east and nothing was going to deflect it. Pressure? Bah. Land? What land? Mountain? Those puny bumps? Charting a path as straight as Mike Pence pretends he is, it was coming for us and no messing. My romantic, fantastic daydreams of apocalyptic weather were suddenly dashed on the rocks of reality. It wasn't just any trees I was going to see bending and bucking and waving like dervishes; it was my trees that tonight, Matthew, would be Kate Bush.

'Right, get out into the garden,' Minori says to me. 'Anything that isn't nailed down, get it in the garage.'

'Everything?'

'Specifically all that crap of yours around the fire pit. Your Greek vases, Asian gods and that fucking robot from that shit TV show.'

'The Cylon from *Battlestar*.'

'Whatever. If we get a call tomorrow from Hasegawa that her kitchen window has been smashed by a flying robot, you can deal with it.'

'Are you going to help?'

'I'll close all the window shutters then I'll come and inspect your work.'

'Yes, boss.'

I love my fire pit. It's the best part of the place, as far as I'm concerned. I guess it's something to do with playing in the woods so much as a kid, and then reading all those Shakespeares where people go into the woods and take ecstasy (as Aaron Sorkin once described A *Midsummer Night's*

Dream), but there's something about mixing indoors and outdoors, something about blending human touches with the natural, something about nature almost, but not quite, overwhelming our attempts at control, that cuts to something deep in me. If I were that way inclined, I'd suspect that maybe in a previous life I'd been an outlaw in a Robin Hood-type gang, at home in the branches, or part of a nomadic tribe on the Steppes, where home was wherever you dropped your bags, but I'm not that way inclined, because, you know, my brain is connected to my spinal cord.

As a child, I spent a lot of time at my grandparents' house in Aberdeenshire. They lived in what had once been the gardener's cottage of a large estate. It was deep in a forest, and whenever I was there I'd run off into the trees, or more usually climb up into them, and not come back until repeatedly called for. There were acres and acres of forest to explore and I knew every inch of it, could run through the thick foliage at full pelt and know where every root and rabbit hole was. We (my sister and my cousins) had tree houses and shelters strewn across the area where we could hide and remain totally hidden, even from irritated parents standing mere metres away. There was one patch where, if you were careful and knew what you were doing, you could cross about a hundred metres of trees and rhododendron without touching the ground. I still remember the sadness that came with realising I had grown too old and too big to scamper through the branches, the limbs bending under my weight. I still love climbing trees today, though a late developed fear of heights has largely hindered that.

Being outside, sitting in the leaves, settling symbiotically into your environment, still gives me a womb-like warmth and my fire pit is the closest I can come to it without actually packing everything in and living in the woods. Around the fire there are Japanese stone lanterns into which, on summer nights, we put lit candles. Above, in the trees, are the Tibetan prayer flags, and at strategic points in the undergrowth and closer to the fire are broken pots, a piece of fossilised tree, a four-brick section of wall and all these little figures: Hawaiian spirits, Aztec gods, a weird surfer, a laughing frog, a Hindu goddess.

This is my church.

But it's an utter pain in the hole when there's a typhoon a-coming.

It takes three wheelbarrow loads to move what are now potential typhoon shrapnel into the garage, and there's also all the bird feeders, the washing poles and a stack of wood that makes excellent kindling and ever better ballistic missiles. I tie the swing to its tree. I take the wooden lid off the old well. I move Lincoln, our surviving pet turtle, inside. It hasn't even started raining yet and already I'm sick to fuck of this typhoon.

By the time it arrives it's dark. I can hear the wind droning outside, the typhoon shutters rattling against the runners. Rain is drilling into the roof and walls like a billion nails trying to get at us. A burst of PA helpfully tells us to remain indoors, as if anyone's listening to Chicken Little's prophecy coming true and thinking, picnic? The TV stations are doing their usual level best to kill off their young reporters by making them stand a few feet from the shoreline without an umbrella so people can get a really good idea of what rain and wind look like. The shutters are annoying me. I want to see, dammit. What's the point of the end of the world if it's happening elsewhere? The lack of visuals makes it worse; the jet engine scream, the random thumps and crashes, the incessant drumming. You can really begin to see how early humans, sheltering in caves, their fire long blown out, would begin to tell stories of angry gods and protective gods, of the beginning and the end of all things, of the need, above all else, to appease this blowy bastard, whoever he is.

Eventually we go to bed. In the morning, it's all sweetness and light. The shutters are thrown back, the windows opened to let the rich air tingle its way through the house. I make a pot of coffee, put Iron & Wine on, and head outside through the open patio doors, settle into a chair and soak in the morning. Coffee in the garden was high on our list when we were looking for land, and it's still a highlight of any day off. I'm keeping the garage door closed for the time being. My re-creation of a ruined temple can wait.

'Iain.' Minori is up on the balcony sweeping debris.

'Aye?'

'Look.'

'Han.'

'What?'

'Look at what?'

'The tree house.'

I wander round the corner of the house with my coffee, the bounce of 'Cinder And Smoke' playing across the garden. The tree house isn't really a tree house, just a tree with a platform between three limbs that the previous owner built for his grandkids. Yoji banned any of his grandkids from playing on it because the tree – a peach tree – looks unsafe. It turns out he was right. The three main limbs of the tree are split, each splayed on the ground in a Mercedes-Benz star.

'Shit.' A quick tour of the garden confirms no other fatalities, and since the deceased is nowhere near my or my neighbours' houses, there's no need for panicked action. I sip my coffee and contemplate a storm that brought down a whole tree. I'd like to have seen that.

'Shit!'

'That's what I said.'

Sasaki comes over, picking debris from between runs of vegetables as he goes. 'A big storm.'

'It was. My first.'

'Is this the only damage?'

'Looks like it. How about your place?'

'Just a mess. No damage. That's what I wanted to talk about.'

'Oh?'

'The sakura trees. Last night the wind bent them right over. They were hitting against my shutters and roof. It was loud, scary. I thought there'd be damage but luckily . . .'

'I'm so sorry. I had no idea the wind would push them that far.'

'Me neither. Typhoons like that never come this way.'

'Thanks for telling me. As soon as I can, I'll cut them back.'

'Oh no, they're so beautiful.'

'I know, but they're only going to get bigger. Next time there might be actual damage.'

'Well, if you insist.'

'I do.' Getting the hang of this indirect diplomacy. 'But it'll have to wait until winter. If we cut them now, while they're still drawing water, they'll get sick and die.'

'We don't want that. They really are very beautiful.'

'No. Hopefully there won't be any more typhoons like that this year.'

'Can you go up that high and cut them down?'

'Nope, but I know a man who can.'

秋

Autumn

Autumn Fallin'

Autumn is by far my favourite time of year. I'm so genetically Northern European that the humidity of an Asian summer puts me into something resembling hibernation. It's one reason I make an effort to travel as much as possible when I'm not working – the heat makes me lethargic and it would be all too easy to spend the long summer vacation under the air conditioner with a slab of cold beer and some movies. Less Netflix and chill, more Netflix and freeze.

The garden feels it too, and the surrounding hills. While the summer heat is a boon to weeds, grass, parasitic vines and other more jungly plants, it's not all that great for the vegetables, flowers and trees. The arrow-straight pine on the eastern edge of my land can never get enough water and by late August is browning more than Elizabeth Barrett, pretty petals wither and crispen, herbs bolt.

So when the temperature begins to get a grip on itself around the end of September, I feel myself waking up, working out, preparing for life. All the clichés of spring – new growth, beginning the cycles, rebirth – that's autumn for me. You can almost see the countryside shiver, shake itself awake, reacquaint itself with the sun as a source of energy, not pain. Rain returns, presaging typhoon season (though that is an increasing misnomer, as climate change pushes the boundaries of the word 'season' like an over-eager chef with a sodium deficiency). The verdancy that until recently predicted a riot of pests and a sweaty, sweary battle with twisting vines and roots buried deeper than a politician's principles returns.

In Scotland, autumn means a couple of months of the most beautiful colours, the hills and forests seemingly on fire with a painter's palette of reds, yellows, browns and golds. Nature puts on its greatest show in what are, effectively, the death throes of the year's growth. Leaves are withering, plants are dying back, everything is shutting down for the impending cold, but by God they're going out with a bang.

There are two distinct planting periods in autumn in Japan. During the dying embers of the summer inferno, it's time for a second planting of broccoli, cauliflower, peppers, cucumber, lettuce, cabbage, peas – the kind of summer crops that can't actually cope with summer. I have no set routine with these vegetables and certainly ignore the biblical stricture to refrain from sowing your field with two kinds of seed. (If the bible is to be taken metaphorically, what is this bit supposed to mean? No threesomes?) A pepper plant here, some rosemary beside it, chillis, a cauliflower. It's haphazard but I've made some interesting discoveries as a result. Peppers grow very well when shaded by taller *shiso* plants. Rosemary and carrots enjoy one another's company. Cucumber and tomato make good bedfellows. Perhaps the farmers of the bible were obsessive compulsive (or compulsive obsessive, which is in alphabetical order).

In Scotland, autumn coincides with the start of the university year, and in Aberdeen that meant a week of guaranteed gorgeous weather seemingly timed to coincide with Freshers' Week. Baby-faced teens escorted by parents already making plans for the newly spare room walk around campus amazed at the stereotype-defying weather. 'Welcome,' Aberdeen says. 'Welcome, come in aboot. Dinnae believe everything you've heard. This isnae the west coast. It disnae ayewis rain here.'

Parents leave. Classes start. The sun dips behind the horizon and stays there until some time around May. It doesn't rain that much in Aberdeen, but holy hell is it windy. Windy and dark and dreich. I think perhaps my love of autumn arises from the twin joys of the first week back at uni and laughing at all those crushed first-year hopes on the first Monday morning when lecture halls fill with moist, steaming Freshers.

Japan has none of this. Academic years begin in April, when the cherry blossom signals the start of the new year, and the burst of beautiful autumn lingers for a fortnight at most. The colours are stunning – the *momiji* (maple) in particular are a breathtaking deep red like the best wine you've ever tasted. And people flock from all over the country to see the autumn leaves in Ise, Kyoto and Korankei. Unfortunately, the season is all too brief. Two weeks at most and the leaves fall, providing excellent fertiliser but less spectacular views.

In those two weeks, temperatures drop from the mid-thirties to the low twenties, maybe even high teens, and it's at times like these that I betray my heritage. In Scotland, 19 degrees is a nice, warm day. Taps aff. But that's because you're approaching 19 degrees from beneath. When 19 means a drop of nearly 20 degrees, 19 is fricking freezing. Autumn, in my ageing years, no longer means the start of term, endless parties and hungover classes, it means pyjamas out, slippers on, and an extra blanket at night. Scots will be mocking me at this point but I am fine with that. I've made my peace. Is anything worn under the kilt? Yes, a hot water bottle and a heat-tech jock strap.

Swallow My Pride

One of the main reasons we wanted to live in the countryside was to become at least partially self-sufficient. I grew up almost in the country-side – right on the edge of the commuter belt – but my grandparents were a bit further out, countryside proper, and they used to grow vege-tables and fruit. Mainly strawberries and peas that mysteriously disappeared from the plant whenever the grandchildren visited. Wild raspberries. Fresh lettuce. It's a cliché but veg from the supermarket really does taste different. Inferior. We've traded taste for convenience.

Minori's grandparents also grew vegetables and rice. We both wanted to get back to that taste, that freedom and that direct contact with how our food is produced.

Which is all very well in theory. Nature is a bit more fickle; it's not as simple as *seed in ground, water, wait, eat.*

When I was at university I wrote a short story inspired by an email that was doing the rounds. I suppose those emails were the precursors to today's memes, viral wit that spreads much like ignorance in the anti-vaccination community. They were frequently racist, sexist, homophobic and often all three. In retrospect we should have seen the writing on the wall for the internet back then but instead we blamed the idiot who forwarded them rather than genetic mutation for not having dealt with this aspect of human nature yet. Anyway, the one I used as the basis for my short story wasn't one of those based on a false assumption about the non-white, non-male, non-straight majority of humanity, rather it was a series of epigrams entitled 'Things I know are true because Hollywood says so'. It contained such gems as 'all bed sheets are

L-shaped, coming up to the neck of the woman but only reaching the waistline of the man', 'people will wait their turn before attacking you' and 'your laptop contains all the hardware and software needed to hack into the systems of any alien civilisation'. The story wasn't great (little I wrote back then was) and it took me a good ten minutes just now digging around my office to find a copy of it, but I was reminded of it that first autumn when I set about preparing the ground for carrots, onions, potatoes and garlic.

Something else I thought was true because Hollywood said so: when someone dies, their friend/killer/jovial local gravedigger can dig a grave six feet down in, like, twenty minutes. Sometimes it's such hard work that they are forced to remove their coat and even, on occasion, to pop their braces off their shoulders and let them hang. Where is this ground made of tofu that's easier to dig than a Miles Davis solo? In reality gravediggers use actual fucking diggers and murder victims are usually so badly buried that a sprightly spaniel has no trouble finding a stray hand shortly after sun-up the next day.

Thanks, Hollywood. Another myth bust.

I put shovel to turf and instantly turned into a ninety-year-old cartoon man.

'Ohhhh, me fookin' back!'

Twenty minutes of heavy panting and heavy swearing and I'd got one wavy trench dug about 20cm deep. I looked across my half an acre.

'The good life, my arse.'

I watched my neighbours, Asai and Sasaki on either side of me. I watched what they did and when they did it. I watched them prepare the ground, perfect geometric trenches and hills. They used cultivators to dig, but then they spent hours out there, bent over, sweating more over each angle than Euclid. Peaks for some plants, plateaux for others. I watched them build runs of Pythagorean beauty and wondered: did it really make a difference to the vegetables? Would a carrot be bigger and better because the slope either side of it was 50 degrees, not 45? Did an onion care if the ground it grew in had been spirit-levelled to within an inch of its life? I knew I didn't.

The problem with learning things by watching men is that men don't often do things for sensible reasons.

The problem is this: men are stupid. Or more correctly, men are, for the most part, stupid (for evidence: see the news. Pick a news story, any news story. I'll wait. Choose one at random and I can guarantee that it could be boiled down to 'stupid man does something stupid and refuses to admit it was his fault'). We can reach great heights, do great things. The 'Great Man' theory of history has some basis in fact, though only some. As the saying goes, we are very much being propped up by a greater woman.

Women can be stupid too – don't get me wrong, I'm an equal opportunities misanthropist – it's just that men, we do it so well. At full force. With all our heart (and little of our brain). We are like Wile E. Coyote. In fact, he may be the perfect personification of male stupidity. We run face first into a tunnel entrance painted onto a cliff face, pick ourselves up, curse the Roadrunner and start all over again. Our brains are like that Pringles ad – once they pop, we can't stop.

My three published novels are, in part, about male stupidity and the first one, *First Time Solo*, is particularly relevant here. It's about men in groups. Men as friends, men as brothers, men as fathers and sons, and men as enemies. That's a lot of dialectical stupidity, a lot of wires getting crossed, a lot of knickers getting twisted and more canned worms than in the bunker of a particularly survivalist early bird.

It all comes down to competition. Whether we are taught it or whether it resides as some vestigial stage of our early evolution, like a kill-switch in our central nervous system that redirects all decision-making to our reptilian brain, it's something that comes naturally and is very hard to fight. From pissing contests in primary school, through every sport ever, to not packing a pillow because *that's not proper camping*, at the first sight of a binary, we can turn anything into a competition. Directions? That's me versus nature, electromagnetism and town planning. To ask is to admit defeat. Instruction manuals? There were no instruction manuals for the wheel. If I can't assemble a bookcase without the aid of diagrams and patronising arrows then I am not worthy of descending from whatever Neolithic genius Edisoned up the wheel. (We have no evidence that it was a man who invented the wheel. I tend to think it's far more likely a woman invented it while a man kept insisting he could carry everything.)

We want to be in control. From one perspective the whole of human history is the attempt to control nature – whether that means to make it unchaotic or to bend it to our will. We are about to reap the results of that folly. Nature is unpredictable. One of the tenets of Eastern philosophy is to accept that fact. Somewhere in the *Tao Te Ching* there is a passage about trying to fight the flow of a river. The rock doesn't fight the flow; it stays where it is and allows the river to flow around it. Getting enraged by incorrect weather forecasts (they are forecasts after all, mathematical predictions based on possibility, not actual facts. If meteorologists really could see into the future I'm sure they'd use their powers for better ends than reminding us to take an umbrella to work tomorrow) or seedlings that just won't sprout or the frustrating and continued existence of caterpillars is as pointless as trying to explain to a campsite manager in Japan that the calendar and the seasons only have an indirect, tenuous relationship.

Anyway. Nature is fine. Survival is a struggle and self-sufficiency is clearly not the easy option. Lawson's wouldn't be called a convenience store for long if you had to raise the chicken, slaughter it, prepare and cook it yourself just to get your nuggets. But that's effectively what we signed up for when we moved out here. Roast potatoes? Here's a shovel, get digging.

It's the competition that gets to me. Even here, even in the entropic face of nature. The men and their competitiveness. The inevitable stupidity of it all.

As I've said before, this village is predominantly elderly. The elderly men grow vegetables. Every spare inch of space on the land is cultivated. And they're great at it. They work from dawn until the heat really kicks in, then they all meet up in front of the sole vending machine for a can of coffee to compare notes. Fertiliser. Tools. Seeds or seedlings. Dates. Weather. As men have done since some shrew-sized mammal stuck its head out from under an asteroid fragment and said, 'It looks like those big lizard things have gone,' they share knowledge and experience.

And brag.

Of course brag.

Whose is the biggest? The longest? It's all a competition, the reptilian brain kicking in. Who has the straightest line on his carrot row? Who has perfect corners on their potato runs? Seriously, these things have right angles and sharp edges. Does a potato really grow better if the ground above it would please a modernist architect?

When did farming get OCD?

When it had too much time on its hands, of course. These men have nothing else to do. They worked hard all their lives and when they retired they came home to a wife they only previously saw on weekends and said, 'Now what?' and she said, 'I don't care but you're not hanging around in here. Out.'

Some of them have part-time jobs. Paper rounds, out on a scooter at 2 a.m. Standing by roadworks with a big flag or a flashing baton. But the garden is theirs.

Asai and Sasaki are no different. All year round their gardens are overflowing with fruit and veg. So much so, that they have to give it away. They all do. They produce so much food they couldn't possibly eat it. Another competition. In the way European monarchs used to discuss potential wives, farmers here discuss whose land is the most fertile, boasting about who has brought the most life into the world.

Example. That autumn, for Minori and me, I planted half a dozen aubergine plants. That did us through the season. By the end of the last one, I was getting a bit sick of them to be honest. Asai, for seven people, planted nearly forty. Ditto for green peppers, celery, basically everything. He doesn't grow what the family needs: he grows what he has space for. Every couple of days I'd come down for work at 6 a.m. and find a basket of vegetables on the doorstep, as lonesome and uninvited as if it were a baby. I don't know how he thought two people could get through food that seven couldn't but every couple of days, another delivery. And next planting cycle, same thing. It was too much. It started to rot. I ended up taking them to work and handing them around, paying it forward. It's pleasing, in a way, and I'm sure he'd be happy if he knew his produce was being enjoyed by a wide range of people he's never heard of.

Everyone is at it. All the old men. There's a cycle of gifting and regifting vegetables, just as there's a cycle of gifting and regifting information.

I put shovel to turf, knowing full well that I couldn't compete. But that sound, the crunch and slice of metal into soil, it's like the bat signal for these people.

'What are you planting there?' Asai is over.

'It's going to be carrots there, potatoes there, garlic and onions.'

'Are you growing the onions from seeds?' Sasaki steps from his patch into mine. 'You're better off buying seedlings straight from Valor.' Asai kicks a clump of mud.

'No, they're too expensive. Kahma does them ten yen cheaper.' Sasaki toes a rock out of the soil.

'Yes, but they're not as sturdy.' Asai rubs his hand towel over his bald head.

'I've never had any problems with them.' Sasaki smiles.

'Anyway, you should soak the soil before digging it.' Asai sits on a stack of bricks I'm saving for a barbecue spot.

'Yeah, and you should at least have done them at five this morning. It's too hot now.'

I stand leaning on my shovel watching them bicker.

'Where did you get that soil from?'

'Over there.' I point. It's the soil I shifted when I built the fire pit. Kind of beige and tan.

'What *taihi* are you using?'

'*Taihi?* What's *taihi?*'

There's a moment of silence. Then they both look around. Walk to the garage and look inside.

'He's not using *taihi*.' The disapproval in Sasaki's voice is severe.

'Maron-kun, come with me. Bring your shovel and the wheelbarrow,' says Asai.

Maron-kun is what he calls me, a familiar diminutive he adopted soon after we moved in. 'Maron' is a shortening of 'Maloney', losing the final syllable and switching the L for the Japanese R (myth busting: the L/R thing isn't an inability to pronounce those sounds, or a confusion between them; rather, in the Japanese language the phonemes *ra*, *re*, *ru*, *re* and *ro* occur in the mouth midway between our L (frontal) and R (near the back)). In other words, there are three sounds fighting for space, not two. I have the exact same issue with the Japanese name 'Ryo' that Japanese speakers have with 'really'. *Kun* is a pet name used for boys; girls get *chan*.

I follow. I trail after him, my barrow rattling across the uneven path. Before Asai's house stands a veritable mountain of compost.

'*Taihi*.'

'Ah.'

'Take some.'

'Thanks.' I shovel three or four piles into the barrow, tentative about how much is acceptable.

'No, no, no.' He takes the shovel from me and heaps it on. Dry black flakes cascade from the mountain in mini avalanches. 'Dump that and come back. Take six more loads.'

'Six? Don't you need it?'

'My cousin makes it. He always gives me too much.'

I bet he boasts about it too.

They stand over me as I mix it with the soil. They say nothing, the atmosphere heavy as I malform irregular, inexact mounds. They shake their heads as I give up, translating the great British motto: it'll do.

When I'm done I get us all some canned coffee and we sit looking over my garden.

'You've got so much space here that you're not using.'

I can hear Asai's thoughts. Waste. A waste of space. He could have grown thousands of onions on this land. Imagine the surplus.

'I have plans for that bit.' I point to the large, flat open area. 'I'm going to dig a series of ponds. Build a gazebo.'

'Like Kagawa's?'

'Bigger.'

You Can't Put Your Arms Around a Memory

Organic farming is very much trial and error. Asai and Sasaki produce lush green fields of vegetables, but it's only when I see Asai in a chemical mask with a spray gun that I realise they are massively cheating. I'm in no hurry and happy with whatever meagre returns I can get.

In front of the house is what the Japanese call a rotary – basically an island around which cars have to drive, a roundabout with only one road, like at the end of a cul-de-sac. You drive onto my land and are funnelled by rocks and trees down what, from above, looks like the long strut of a lowercase D. You turn at the bottom, loop round and exit the way you came in. Pausing, presumably, to visit us. The island is marked top and bottom by two plum trees and outlined by railway sleepers, making it basically immovable, much to Minori's chagrin. My tiny Suzuki Hustler (more on which later) can sweep round the loop in one fluid motion. Her longer Honda can't make it, requiring a touch of reversing and repositioning. She'd like the island gone but not the plum trees. No can do.

The island quickly becomes my testing ground. It's divided in two equal halves by a railway sleeper though it takes me a while to work this out since when we moved in the entire thing was overgrown with mint. Enough mint to keep Hemingway in mojitos for an entire weekend. A minty forest. It took us two days to tire of mint. My friend Luci came up with a bottle of rum. We abandoned mojitos quickly and just started adding Coke. The mint had to go.

'How do you kill mint?' Minori asked.

'Spear it?' I offered to silence.

I hauled it up by the roots but it's sturdy stuff. A few weeks later it's back, mocking me and my hard work like it took offence at the spearmint pun. I try again. And again. My weekends are peppered with attempts to rid my island of its minty-fresh pest. The burning summer heat seems to do the work for me, and by September I'm looking at rich tilled soil ready for me to try and err.

Half I turn into a herb garden: rosemary for meaty dishes (or remembrance, as Ophelia would have it, if memory serves), basil (screeched in Sybil Fawlty's voice at all times), thyme, which we're constantly running out of, lemongrass which fails to survive Minori breaking and smelling it every time she comes out the door, and cilantro for literally everything (I love cilantro though it is hugely unpopular in Japan, where many people call it 'too spicy', oddly), and red *shiso* which is purple and blue *shiso* which is green.

The Japanese language has a strange relationship with colour. For a long time they didn't acknowledge green, and everything of that hue was labelled blue. Even after inventing the word *midori* to describe green things, blue still dominates. Traffic lights are red, yellow and blue, apparently. Forests are blue. Kermit, presumably, finds it not easy being blue, which casts that whole song in a more melancholy light.

The other half I give over to vegetables I suspect are difficult. In a sense, I am prejudiced and divide veg into two camps: above ground and below ground. Eloi and the Morlocks, if you will. The ones below ground, the Morlocks, I can understand them. Put potato into the right kind of ground. Leave. Dig up more potatoes than you put in. One potato, two potato and so on. Above ground, they require maintenance, they require tending, they are needy and annoying, demanding constant attention, kind of like children except you can eat them once they are fully grown, and if they get sick you can leave them to rot on the compost heap. (I don't have kids, so I'm just speculating, but I'm pretty sure Swift was joking about the eating, and composting our young is frowned upon even though it is better, environmentally speaking, than chemical fertilisers.) Tomatoes are, figuratively, a pain in the hole. Cucumbers and peas require the building of structures up which they can clamber. Lettuces need nets and are nothing more than bug magnets, which, if I'm not cheating, I can't do much about without spray.

What's the worst that can happen? So I dig. I build. I plant. I am surprisingly successful. Handfuls of cherry tomatoes. Big fat cucumbers that Minori douses in sesame oil and chilli peppers. This is literally my favourite thing at the moment. If you take nothing else from this book, take this: batons of cucumber in sesame oil, fish *dashi* and chilli peppers. It's what taste buds evolved for.

But the victory is the peas. When I was a child, my grandfather grew row after row of peas and, unlike the town of Taiji in Mie, never harvested a single pod. His grandchildren (and his children it must be said) went at them like locusts upon ancient Egypt, zombies upon a half-shut gate, or me upon a free bar. Fresh peas from the pod is one of those sense memories I will carry to the grave, like new sawdust or melting tarmac on a hot day. A smell and taste so evocative Proust could have bored the arse off half of France for decades with that alone. Every morning I pick a few and eat them at the traffic lights. Stray peas roll under the seats and I fantasise about them taking root, filling my car with pea vines, like some Ghibli-esque miracle, but they turn black and I find them a month later while searching for all the coins Newton took from me.

The peas sprout and grow. One day I notice a few of the pods have been chewed by something and, since the temperature is starting to turn, I take this as a sign to pick the rest of the crop. I fill a muffin box with peas (we shop at Costco, and their muffins come in a big plastic tub, which could easily be replaced by something more environmentally friendly but they do come in handy at harvest time, being just the right size and strong enough to not buckle under the weight of produce) and take them in after work and have a few, but they don't really go with the penne all'Arrabbiata (you'll need a tray) so I leave them overnight. The next day I pop a pod. They are crunchy and bitter. So are the next ones. And the next.

I've left them too long. I left them hanging, admiring my own skill, the beauty of what I brought forth from the ground and now, like me on a lazy Sunday, they are needlessly wasted.

There's some trite moral here about memory and the past and how you can't go back, but I don't want to go down that Proustian road: a *Swann's Way* can break your arm so I'll just leave this episode with this thought: don't leave things too long, as you may miss your chance. If you need a pea, have one.

Anybody Wanna Take Me Home?

Minori and I had only been going out a few months when we moved to Scotland together. It wasn't planned that way, just a confluence of events which at the time, to us, seemed fine, but whenever I begin explaining to others seems a touch chaotic, like Brexit from a Tory perspective, or a third season with José Mourinho.

She'd been planning to go to the UK and study English, saving her pennies and cramming at the language school. I was approaching the end of my second year – as were the friends I'd started with: Francis, Mitchell, Thom, Jen. Thom left first, in the new year of 2007, Jen not long after, and Francis and Mitchell were planning their exits when our contracts were up in June, both heading to Australia. John, my first boss, had gone, Darius, my Kiwi flatmate, had gone. It was beginning to look a lot like I'd be back at square one, friendship-wise. I was considering my own options. Minori and I had known each other for more than a year, but the relationship was still young and I wasn't sure if Japan was for me long-term. I'd put a request in to transfer to Hiroshima the previous summer, but nothing had come of it and I'd almost forgotten when, in February, it came through. At the same time, my mother announced that she'd be getting remarried in the April. Then Minori's visa was granted, all within a few weeks. Decision: I'd go back for the wedding and find a flat in Edinburgh. Minori would follow. She'd study; I'd deal with the nasty business of Britain's services and see for myself whether I was destined to be abroad long-term, or if I'd got it all out of my system and was ready to go home.

Spoiler: we didn't even last the full twelve months. Edinburgh was amazing, but it took me nine months to get anything other than temp work so I racked up a load of debt, Minori couldn't get any work other than part-time casual jobs because of visa restrictions, and the casual racism she encountered was the deciding factor.

Scene: Minori is walking by a building site near Fountainbridge. A call from high atop the scaffold.

Builder: *Ni hao! Ni hao!* Why don't you fuck off back to China?

Minori: Why don't you fuck off back to England?

Before we left Japan, back in March 2007, there was the small factor of meeting the parents. We'd been dating since November, so this was way too soon to contemplate anything that drastic, but understandably they were loth to let their eldest disappear halfway around the world with some guy they'd never clapped eyes on. So it was arranged. Dinner, their place, after work one night.

Shitting. An absolute. Brick.

Minori picked me up from work, her younger sister, Chiharu, standing by the car in the car park.

'NICE TO MEET YOU!' she shouted from a good twenty feet away. I get in the back and Chiharu turns round, fixes me with a mischievous look. 'You love my sister, yes?'

Fortunately, that was the extent of her English. No one else spoke a word of anything other than Japanese, so my stuttered, mumbled, baffled replies were filtered through Minori. Everyone was home: both her parents, brother Kingo, and Haru, Kingo's son from his first marriage, then three years old. They sat me down at the table and Yoji plied me with beer while Miyoko produced a seemingly endless supply of food until I felt like a drunken Augustus Gloop. There's a major disconnect here between Scottish and Japanese culture. In Scotland, you are taught to clear your plate, eat everything up because there are starving people in Africa and your mother didn't slave over a hot stove just to have it thrown in the bin, so you're going to sit there and eat every last morsel. In Japan, if your guest clears their plate, it reflects badly on the hostess: perhaps you may have eaten more, the thinking goes. Obviously she didn't prepare enough food. Bad hostess, shame on you.

No one told me this. No one told her. The more she served, the more I ate. I was ready to burst but more fried chicken, another bowl of soup, some more fish. I eventually had to embrace impoliteness and give up – not clearing your plate is better than vomiting all over it. Part of me is curious to see how far she would have gone: if I could have eaten the house empty, if she had a wafer-thin mint somewhere that would have finished me off, if she would ever have caved in to reality over cultural expectations.

Miyoko tried to engage me in conversation through Minori.

'She wants to know who asked out who.'

'I asked Minori out.'

Miyoko paused, strained recall on her face. 'Propose?'

I damn near spat out a piece of pork.

Minori collapsed in laughter and her mum looked confused, returned to the kitchen. Her brother made his apologies, getting ready to leave.

'Where is he going?'

'Practice. He's a volunteer fire-fighter.'

In Japanese, I say that my father was a fireman.

'Volunteer or full-time?'

I fumbled the grammar and somehow managed to imply that my father was a 'proper' fireman. This didn't go down well and I got to practise my apologies.

After dinner Minori invited me up to see her room and in doing so successfully completed my transition from twenty-six-year-old teacher to gibbering teenager. We climbed the stairs, nearly flattened by a rampaging Haru, who after an evening hiding behind the sofa had suddenly decided that this was the time to get to know me. He pulled all his toys from his room into hers, handed me his English picture dictionary and said he wanted to study. 'Banana' and 'potato' later, he sodded off. By this point I was exhausted and it was time to leave. Miyoko produced a doggie-bag with enough leftovers to keep Napoleon's army going through most of Russia.

*

To be fair, I got off lightly. Chiharu married her childhood sweetheart, Shinya. He comes from a very old-fashioned family, and despite having dated Chiharu for a decade, his father made him ask Yoji for her hand in the traditional Japanese way. The day before he went down on two knees, Miyoko called up Minori.

'Are you both free tomorrow?'

'I think so. Why?'

'You have to come over. Shinya's going to ask if he can marry Chiharu. It's going to be hilarious.'

The poor man had to go through the ritual, down on his knees, prostrating himself before Yoji, with the entire family looking on. I'm only surprised Miyoko didn't hand out popcorn.

I did have my own horrifying moment with Yoji before Minori and I got married and, as you'd guess, it was language-based.

In winter, Japanese people like to eat *oden*. It is a kind of hotpot dish with things like boiled eggs, *daikon* (radish) and fishcakes served in a soy broth. It's warming on a cold day and is sold at most convenience stores. One of the ingredients is *konnyaku*, a jelly-like . . . thing that resembles the kind of congealed gloop you find behind an old fridge. Everyone else loves it, I can't stand the stuff.

A few months before we got married we were round at her parents' house. Miyoko had prepared *oden* and I was passing bits of *konnyaku* to Minori. The conversation was flowing around me as it often does – like all families they were talking of people they all know, shared memories, things that I couldn't understand even if I knew every word and grammatical form they were using, something I didn't at the time. People often forget that understanding the language is only half the battle. I can understand every word you say but if you're talking about something I've never heard of, or have no experience of, I'm not going to be able to take part in the conversation. We all have grandparents who talk about people who died years before we were born but expect us to know them. Imagine that combined with a whole other language and culture.

Anyway, I wasn't paying much attention to the chat, just focusing on getting all that rubbery crap out of my bowl, when Yoji says, 'How do you feel about *konnyaku*?'

I look up. 'Sorry, but I really can't stand it. It's the feeling, it makes me feel . . .' And I shudder, unable to find the word for that feeling.

He looks shocked, a little angry. Something I've never seen before in this placid man. Everyone else is pissing themselves laughing.

I turn to Minori. 'What?'

She answers in Japanese. 'He asked how you feel about *konnyaku*.'

'Yes.' This time I notice something is wrong with the grammar. They are using *konnyaku* as a verb and have turned it into the present tense. I am *konnyaku*-ing? What the fuck does that mean? '*Konnyaku?*' I say, lifting some with my chopsticks. 'I don't like it.'

Renewed laughter, this time from Yoji as well.

'No,' says Minori, in English this time. 'Not *konnyaku*, *kon-yaku*. There's a small "tsu" after the "n". Can you hear the difference?'

'Not really, no. What does it mean?'

'To be engaged. He asked you how you feel about marrying me.'

Public Service Announcement

Historically Japan has been something of a militaristic society. There is a period of history specifically labelled the Age of Warring States (Sengoku Jidai, 1467–1600); samurai and ninjas are two of the most exportable aspects of Japanese culture; and the Edo Period (1600–1868) is chiefly remarkable for being a period of sustained peace on the archipelago.

Militarism returned through the First Sino-Japanese war (1894–1895), the Russo-Japanese War (1904–1905), the First World War (Japan was a British ally in that war, and on the request of Britain invaded the German colonies in China, which included the Tsingtao Brewery) and the Second Sino-Japanese War which escalated into the Second World War. Since then, Japan has eschewed war (apart from some logistical support whenever the US demanded it) but some remnants of that authoritarian, militaristic culture survive to this day.

I mentioned in the second chapter, 'Who by Fire', that there is a First World War memorial in the forest near our home. In Britain and most countries, I'd imagine, that would be pretty unremarkable, but in Japan war memorials are unusual, for obvious reasons. What is more common are school uniforms that deliberately resemble naval uniforms (black uniforms for boys, blue-and-white sailor suits for girls. I'll give you one guess which section of society picked those outfits). There's a fair amount about modern Japanese schooling that hints at its past: marching, flags, military music pumped out during sports days, mandatory crew cuts for all members of the baseball team. I've asked a number of school teachers about this and every single one has responded with some variation of: 'We hate it. But the grandparents like it, so it stays.' To be fair, the answer to most questions along the line of 'Why is X done that way?' will have something to do with the elderly, who, at the time of writing, make up a third of the population (33 per cent are over sixty) though in my village I reckon it's somewhere nearer 97 per cent.

The other major hangover is the public address system. Our area has one and it serves two functions. The first I've never got used to and can't help considering somewhat fascistic – in the sense that it was put in place by actual fascists. It may sound innocuous to some, and most Japanese people I've spoken to about it can't understand what I'm getting all worked up about, but I stand by my reaction. What I'm talking about is the twelve and five o'clock alarms. At twelve o'clock, on the dot, the local part-time fire station lets rip with a blast of air-raid siren. Why they do it at twelve, why it would be the fire brigade's responsibility, and why no one ever tells them to pack it in is beyond me. But there it is, every day, weekday and weekend. *It's twelve o'clock*.

I should say, I have no problem with church or temple bells – one of the temples nearby bongs at seven every morning and I love it. It's a better way to start the day than an iPhone alarm. (Not that anyone around here is still abed at seven – by Christ it's nearly lunchtime!) But the siren really gets my back up. Not half as much as the five o'clock jingle though. Five o'clock, a tinny muzak version of some classical melody I've never been able to place is broadcast like influenza across the skies. *It's five o'clock*.

Why do they get to me so? It's not the noise, and I wouldn't like it any better if the air-raid siren was replaced with 'Living On A Prayer' and the five o'clock muzak changed to an excerpt from the collected speeches of Malcolm X. It's not the intrusion itself, it's the rationale behind it.

It's twelve o'clock. We all – every single last one of us – eat lunch at twelve o'clock. It's twelve o'clock. Time to eat lunch. This means you.

Now it's five o'clock. GO HOME! It's time to be at home, not anywhere else. If you are anywhere other than home, be prepared to explain why.

*

It's the uniformity, the assumed homogeneity of action and intention that terrifies me. It's the acceptance that someone – anyone – has the authority to regulate the time when you eat lunch *at home*.

Obviously that's not how most people here consciously view it. It's something that's been there for generations, a clue for kids in a time when there were no watches or phones, but what's it still doing here? What purpose does it serve beyond a brief burst of nostalgia and scaring the crap out of me? Some say it's just testing the system in case of an emergency – run, run, the quakes are coming, but why test it in this way, at these times, every damn day? If you tested a fire alarm like this, people would be throwing wolves at it.

The second use of the PA is much more understandable. In a society where the elderly are a significant demographic and increasing all the time (though as the birth rate is dropping, this position is clearly untenable and will sort itself out in the end), and where generations tend to live under one roof and are often cared for at home (though this too is changing with the generations), biddies with dementia going AWOL is a constant hazard.

Once a fortnight or so – more in the summer (even those suffering from dementia don't fancy the winter cold) – a ping-PING-pong echoes around the village followed by some variation of:

Good morning. This is the Community Association. A person has gone missing. An eighty-six-year-old woman. She is wearing brown trousers, a red cardigan and a black overcoat. She was last seen at five a.m.... Message repeats.

The short sentences are to take into account the echo and sound-wave degradation caused by the thing being turned up *way too fucking loud*. I've never worked out if it's to compensate for the average age of the listeners or if it's something ingrained – the music and announcements over the kindergarten's PA are audible miles away. It's like every public official given access to a loudspeaker immediately turns into Nigel Tufnel. It's so up to eleven that nine times out of ten I can't make out an eighth of what they're saying.

This is a long-standing problem with me, and one reason, I suspect, why my Japanese isn't as good as it should be after all this time. There's something wrong with the connection between my ears and the part of my brain that understands speech. I first noticed it at football games, where the chants of the crowd are completely incomprehensible, just one long undulated gruff exhalation. Everyone else seems to get it, but I'm as in the dark as a myopic miner. I still have no idea what the songs are at Nagoya Grampus and just make up my own words so I can sing along. One song the fans sing is helpfully to the tune of Offspring's 'Why Don't You Get A Job?' so I just go with that. Another, I'm pretty sure I'm wrong in saying, goes: '*In Nagoya,* いい唐揚げ.' (In Nagoya, good fried chicken.) It often happens in moments of stress. I guess my brain goes: 'Here, this is important. Pay attention.' Unfortunately, that inner monologue runs over the top of the other person speaking. It's a self-perpetuating cycle, like a hipster's Penny Farthing powered by smugness.

Brain: Right, this time pay attention.

Other person: So, what do you think?

Me: Goddammit.

Anyway, the echo and fragmentation, combined with whatever this psychological hearing disorder is, means I often miss the gist of the announcements.

The missing people tend to be found pretty quickly. Usually, they've wandered a little bit off the beaten path and exasperated relatives take advantage of the PA rather than going to look for them. I know for sure that's what happened one night when the announcement that two teenagers – a boy and a girl – hadn't returned by their curfew. There was much ribald guffawing at this the next day, and you can be damn sure the young couple didn't lose track of time again.

Occasionally, an announcement in our neck of the woods is broadcast to other villages and, very occasionally, across the entire area. The split-second delays mix with the echoes to turn the whole thing into a tinny mush. The only time this has happened since we moved in, I couldn't even tell what language they were using. It sounded like a whale attempting Klingon. Fortunately, Minori was with me.

'There's been a murder.'

We lived in Scotland for a year, and Minori has picked up a few things. Mostly swear words, but occasionally something like this.

'Thank you, Taggart. Wait . . . what?'

'Someone tried to rob a convenience store and stabbed the clerk. They're on the run.'

'Oh.' I look around our garden, the wider village. One end is all forest and hills, little shrines, temple buildings, a campsite on the other side. Garages, *kuras* (traditional Japanese storehouses), the warehouse at the wrecker's yard, and quite a few abandoned houses. If I were on the run, where would I hide? 'We should go inside and lock the door.'

'Why?'

'If it were me, I'd hide in our garage.'

'Yeah, but you live here. That's the first place they'd look and you'd be caught.'

'No, I mean if I were him instead of me, I'd hide at mine.'

'What? Anyway he's nowhere near here.'

'Presumably he's in a car though. He could get here quickly. If it were me, I'd ditch the car up that dirt track by the shrine and go through the forest.'

'Yeah, maybe.'

She seems unfazed by all of this. Japan is *safe*. These things aren't supposed to happen here. I've become sensitised to crime by all the safety. If this were Glasgow I'd shrug, glance out the window and get on with my day. Here, I've got the net curtains twitching and I'm fantasising about murderers in my crawl space.

Ping-PING-pong. *He's been sighted heading east.*

We're west. I feel a little let down. It's a bit like early radio, like *The War of the Worlds*, hanging on for the next instalment. Whodunnit? Will he get away? Will they ever find the one-armed man? What happens if they get into a high-speed pursuit OJ-style? Will they describe it over the PA? Maybe these things aren't so bad after all. Inevitably, entertainment will win out.

That night I check the cupboards and crawl spaces for hidden maniacs. It's something else to add to the list after snakes, centipedes and wild boar.

Talking World War III Blues

After the North Korean missile test in August 2017, I catch myself fantasising about World War Three.

Sitting in my garden with the fire sparking and the birds telling me to get lost out of their territory, I wonder what I would do if war were declared, if the sirens sounded and the J-Alert sent me running. Would I run straight to the airport, abandoning any pretence that this is now my home, not that other island 5,000 miles away? Would I stay, stick it out, show solidarity.

Birds drop from the branches, grab at worms, insects, seeds, and reclaim their swaying vantage. What would I actually do if North Korea attacked?

I've read too much history. I've read so many books about war, about camps, about conscription, about conscientious objection. How would I be treated if Japan went to war? How would I behave? In the last war foreigners were rounded up, interned in Kobe or sent to Shanghai, the colour of their hair, the shape of their nose enough to make them suspect. Of course it happened everywhere – what's war, and the US border, without camps, fences and barbed wire? But would it happen again? It would to some, but would I be included? How would I react? You can't know until you're there. You can't know your true self, the real you huddled inside your head, until you've been tested by something that pricks the bubble of your existence, a zero-sum situation. Maybe that's why most veterans don't talk about it. They didn't like what they found, when layers and layers were stripped away and the kernel of identity was revealed; they didn't like how it looked, how it tasted. Or maybe they just know that we could never understand, not having been exposed ourselves.

This is what I ponder, in my garden with the ripped edges of Mount Ontake framed between two *matsu* pine trees. If I fled, if I took Minori with me back to Scotland, she'd be a refugee. Her family suffering while she's safe. I take a beer from the cooler box, the wind whipping the overgrown lemongrass plant.

I asked Kingo, Minori's brother, if he'd fight. North Korea had launched a missile, or China was sounding off about some island or other that day, I forget which provocation was on the news.

'Of course.'

'Even if you disagree with the war? If you disagree with the government and feel no ill will to the other side? You'd still go?'

'Of course.'

'I couldn't. I wouldn't. I'd rather go to prison.'

'And then what would they do to your wife? To your family?'

I chewed on a piece of *maguro sashimi* and didn't answer.

What answer could I give? I don't have a family. We don't have a family, Minori and me. It's just Minori and me. Would I die – would I kill – to save her from persecution?

Or would I fly?

It's impossible to know how you'd react in extreme situations. There's no real way to prepare, to steel yourself against something your body can't envision. I sometimes jump when the toaster pops.

Sometimes I think I'm preparing myself. The news is so bad, every day, that something cataclysmic seems inevitable. Maybe if I obsess over it now, I'll take it in my stride when it finally happens.

Sometimes I want it to happen. All this posturing by politicians, all this hatred fired up in a populace purely to distract from domestic failures. Domestic failures. Problems at home. Maybe a bomb would sort it all. I could worry about the concrete present instead of potential futures.

All that wasted energy, all that fear and anxiety, about things that never happen.

Such Great Heights

In Scotland I always associate my favourite season with the start of a new university year, with friends returning from their hometowns, with parties, new classes and a feeling of renewal. Basically, what everyone else associates with spring, I have transferred to autumn. I didn't enjoy school at all, and the summer of 1998, when I finished sixth year and moved to university, is something of an Etch A Sketch moment in my life. Shake and erase. I like to say I cut myself off from everyone and began a new life, became a new person, but in reality there wasn't really anyone to cut myself off from. There's a scene in *Red Dwarf* where Rimmer is leaving the crew for a better life on a holographic ship. In his parting speech he tells his former crew mates: 'I have come to regard you as people I once met.' So with my former classmates. There was no closeness on either side, I don't miss them, and on their part my absence from reunions won't be noted. September 1998 marks the moment when Iain Maloney was born again, hence autumn forever being the season of regeneration in my imagination.

Autumn in Japan is both more heightened and more disappointing than in Scotland. After the swampy heat of the summer it is a welcome return to comfort and the ability to go more than three hours without a shower or change of clothes. Japanese maple leaves are the very definition of gorgeous as they change from lush light green through russet to a deep amber. Unfortunately, like a Trump speech, once the temperature goes over the edge, it'll keep plummeting. There's a two-week window when, for me at any rate, it's perfect. The Goldilocks season. Then it's 4 degrees in the morning, ice on the windows and taking the turtle in when it gets dark.

*

New season, new chance to serve the community. At the start of October there's another go around the neighbourhood, waking and walking on a Sunday morning with fellow hungover men, protecting the streets from wind-borne litter, and this time, with hoes, weeding the side of the road and any public paving. With the recent typhoons, this is slightly more necessary than normal. At the end of October, it was our turn on the rota to clean the community meeting hall. This is a woman's job, and usually an elderly woman's job, but as Minori will be taking on the *hanchō* role in 2019, every other task falls to me. For the morning, I am an honorary elderly woman in our small town.

Our village shares a community meeting hall with two or three nearby villages and a cleaning rota is in force. Again, as everyone cleans up after themselves anyway this is more for show. Since it's all an act, I gave some serious thought to dressing up like a Monty Python old lady but I'm pretty sure 'The Batley Townswomen's Guild Presents the Battle of Pearl Harbour' has never made it to leafy Gifu and even surer it wouldn't find a receptive audience.

I meet Mrs Hasegawa and Mrs Sasaki outside their homes and together we stroll to the hall. I say stroll. Mrs Sasaki is one of those Japanese women ravaged by osteoporosis. I used to teach English to an orthopaedic surgeon and he said that education about osteoporosis was one of Japanese medicine's biggest failures. Looking at Mrs Sasaki's perpendicular spine I couldn't help but agree he had a point.

Being a man, the two women assume basic cleaning is beyond me. I am tasked with opening the typhoon shutters that are permanently closed and then grudgingly handed a vacuum cleaner and watched with suspicion as I push it across the carpet, unplugging and replugging the tiny cable every few metres. Mrs Hasegawa tackles the toilet while Mrs Sasaki gets down on her knees and pushes a wet cloth along the non-carpeted parts of the floor. I offer to do that for her, but she waves me away with an irritated flap. Her bones may not be strong but her will certainly is, and her temper's shorter than the vacuum cable. Reluctantly, I leave her to it. I pack away the vacuum and ask Mrs Hasegawa what to do next.

'Nothing. You can go. I know you're busy. Thanks for your help.'

'No, no, I'm not going home and leaving you both here. We're a team.'

She laughs at this, though whether it's the idea that I'm on their team or that I'm in any way helpful is unclear.

'Can I use this?' I take a spare cloth, wet it in the kitchen and go around the room wiping the tops of the picture and door frames, the air conditioners and light shades. Clearly this has not been done for a long time. From about 170cm down, the room is immaculate. Above that, there are cobwebs and clumps of dust that look almost like the dust bunnies in the *Totoro* movie. I half expect one to blink at me. I'm a little disappointed that none of them do.

I can hear the women chatting.

'He's really tall.'

'Yes. I guess that's useful for jobs like this.'

'I could do with someone like that in my house. For lightbulbs and things.'

'His wife is lucky. The bulb in my toilet blew and I had to wait until the weekend for my son to come and change it.'

'I don't think my husband has ever changed a lightbulb.'

'You should have married a foreigner. He hangs out the washing every day. I've seen him.'

'No, I couldn't have married a foreigner. What would I cook?'

'True.'

We pack up and saunter home. Mrs Sasaki invites us in for tea and to show off her new fence. We sit in her *tatami* room sipping the green tea that grows in her garden while they ask me *taberaremasu ka?* about every item of food they can think of. It's relaxed and fun, much more so than the forced chat over coffee cans in the summer. I think I prefer being an honorary old lady.

I finish my tea and just as I'm getting ready to leave, Mrs Sasaki points to a floor-to-ceiling cupboard.

'Before you go, could you help me with something . . .'

The Shy Retirer

When I first moved, I was running my own English conversation school in Ichinomiya, a sleeper town orbiting Nagoya. The drive from my new home to work was prohibitive but I wasn't in a position to pack it in. Moving is expensive: settling old bills, racking up new ones, all these hidden taxes that suddenly land on the mat, all that beer and comfort food to help fight the stress don't come cheap. By the end of September, I felt I was ready to close down the school and reopen it in my freshly painted *tatami* room. I printed hundreds of flyers and delivered them to the letterboxes of everyone in my village and a handful of neighbouring ones. I built a website, made up business cards, opened a new email address and waited.

And waited.

I opened my original school with half a dozen students and figured that since I wouldn't be paying rent on a classroom, I only needed a couple to get the ball rolling. Well, the ball refused to roll. The Asais took a flyer, asked me some questions, suggested to their eldest who was just about to start junior high school that she might benefit from having a tutor next door.

'No.'

'Why.'

'Just no.'

'She's embarrassed.'

'I just don't want to.'

Seems my neighbours were happy to teach me about growing vegetables, caring for the community and fitting in, happy to sit round my fire and chat, but were less keen for me to tutor their children. Minori reckoned it was a money thing. I suspect that while the adults were curious about this weird new novelty in the village, the children were much more circumspect.

One of the odder stereotypes Japanese people have of themselves is that they are shy. I say odd because usually your stereotypes about yourself are positive. The British tend to use adjectives like fair, friendly and polite, traits that are clearly universal in every country and just as clearly often absent. As a result, shyness is given a positive spin in Japan. When they say they are shy, they often mean in comparison with Americans. The loud, blustery, forceful image of the average American is used as a counterpoint against which the Japanese define themselves and thus quiet, demure shyness can become a virtue. The problem is it becomes self-fulfilling. Japanese are shy. To be Japanese is to be shy. Therefore, shyness isn't to be discouraged. 'Ah, she's shy!' is said of kids in the same tone as 'Ah, she's cute!' or 'Ah, she's clever!'

Both my nieces were shy around me to the point of offence. Shima and Ao are currently in elementary school, but each girl, between the ages of two and four, would cry when I entered the house, run away, hide, scream and generally refuse to behave themselves. Rather than being scolded for this ridiculous behaviour, it was tolerated, laughed at, treated as if it was only natural. It isn't natural. It's attention-seeking behaviour that they clearly felt was being rewarded. And it was hurtful. I became reluctant to visit my in-laws during these years. When Minori's brother had another child, Miki, I dreaded another two years of this nonsense, but fortunately – or perhaps as a result of entrenched gender expectations, Miki being a boy – he wasn't as shy or wasn't praised for it and so didn't pursue the behaviour.

Shyness is one of those traits I have little patience for, because I suffered from it myself. As a child I had two extremes: introverted or hyperactive. I went on a school skiing trip to France when I was thirteen. I was the only one from my year on the trip, and the youngest by a couple of grades. On the bus from Aberdeen to the airport I said nothing. In the airport I spoke to no one. One girl took pity on me and drew me out of my shell, got me talking. By the time we arrived in France I'd talked so much that I overheard her say to her friend, 'Christ, I preferred him when he was silent.' The ley lines of those characteristics have underpinned my adulthood. Few who know me now think of me as shy or introverted, but that's because I made a conscious, terrible effort to overcome it.

Moving to Japan was, in one sense, a jump from the headland, a way of forcing myself to defeat the Balrog of shyness once and for all, and to a large extent it worked. Besides which, if you're built like a rugby player that's gone to seed, no one believes for one second that you are shy. Introversion in the large is interpreted as surly, arsey passive-aggression. People I've known for decades will be reading this and scoffing, 'Him? That noisy fucker, introverted? My arse.' Never underestimate the power of defence mechanisms and alcohol to mask inner insecurities. The way I interact with the world and the way the world interacts with me has always been founded on a misunderstanding, partly based on appearances and partly based on pretence on my part, and the gap between my understanding of myself and the image others have of me has long been a source of deep pain.

In short, shyness can be overcome; confidence can be faked and made. All too often in Japan, shyness is acceptable and cute, the way a snaggle-tooth on a woman is often considered sexy, or insensitive self-ishness is taken as being manly behaviour in a husband. All can be fixed, but only if there is a will to do so.

For kids, being shy is enough to get them out of doing things they don't want to do, a catch-all excuse that parents can't counter. Only a couple of weeks before writing this, Ueda-san, a mother from the other side of the village, turned up at my door asking me to tutor her sixteen-year-old son. I agreed, and gave her my phone number, prices and a sketched outline of the curriculum. A few days later she sent me the following email:

. . . I want him to study with you. He wants to go to a good university and become a programmer, but his English grades aren't good enough. I fought with him but he says he's too embarrassed [another way of saying shy] *to come.*

The trump card. He won that fight.

I suspect this is a large part of the reason why that first autumn I didn't get a single enquiry regarding lessons. Something else happened that autumn that put me off closing down my school in Ichinomiya. There was a big problem with the bathroom.

My brother-in-law, Kingo, is a carpenter. In Japan most buildings and almost all houses are made from wood, the Three Little Pigs never having had the kind of literary, philosophical and architectural influence they enjoyed in Europe. This is primarily due to the perpetual threat of earthquakes. In brief, the thinking is that either you pay a huge amount of money to make your house earthquake-proof or you accept that a big earthquake (the big ones are rare) will bring your house down – and wood causes less destruction and costs less to clear up than stone. In the event of a smaller earthquake doing damage, wood is also easier to repair.

By the same logic, a straw house would be better than a wooden one, but the Three Little Pigs didn't have typhoons to deal with. Fairy tales rarely have much in the way of climactic realism. A house made of cake and candy? In a forest in Germany? On a hot day your roof caramelises, and at the first sign of rain you're going to be able to make more soggy bottom jokes than the average series of *Bake Off*.

So in Japan, when you say someone is a carpenter, you mean they are a builder. Kingo builds houses.

At some point, and I can't for the life of me remember why, he stuck his head through the hatchway in the cupboard under the stairs.

'I see water.'

'Water? Like damp?'

'No, like puddles.'

'That's not good, is it?'

'Not usually, no.'

Kingo and I have a kind of dislocated relationship. We have exactly nothing in common, no shared interest or experiences, no similar pursuits or contiguous epistemologies. A conversational détente has developed between us where we are perfectly pleasant with each other but never actually talk about anything. Suddenly we have a topic.

'Where's that coming from?'

'I need to go down and see.'

I pull out the climbing head-torches, he gets a spare boiler suit from his car (yes, he's the kind of man who has a spare boiler suit just in case), and we clamber into the crawl space beneath the floor.

My first thought is centipedes, snakes, spiders and what other manner of leggy nastiness might be lurking there. Then I bang my head and forget all about it. For the same geological reasons mentioned above, Japanese houses don't have basements, so there's less than a metre of clearance. This necessitates hands-and-knees perambulation. There's a lot of water, a worrying amount. We get our bearings in relation to the rooms overhead. The toilet is here, the sink here, so the dividing wall is here, the bath and shower here, the sink here, washing machine here. Lots of potential sources of water.

'*Ee? Baka!*' WTF? Ridiculous!

'What is it?'

'Look.'

I crawl over to where he's pointing. 'What am I looking at?'

'We're under the bath.'

'Yeah.'

'Can you see what's wrong?'

'It's wet.'

'Apart from that.'

'I'm not sure.'

'What's missing?'

'Um. Dryness? I don't know.'

Plumbing is not my thing. I've no idea what the underside of a bath is supposed to look like, I've never even pondered what it may look like, so I can't begin to imagine what I'm actively not seeing.

'It's obvious.'

Not to me.

'When you pull the plug, where does the water go?'

'Down.'

'Down what?'

'A pipe.'

'Exactly.'

'Exactly what?'

'There's no pipe.'

To be fair, that should have been obvious, even to me.

There never had been a pipe. For nineteen years this house had stood and at no time had the bath been plumbed in. Every bath ever taken by the previous owners had flooded the foundations. Now, Japanese people bathe daily. For those who haven't experienced it, a brief explanation. A Japanese bathroom is a large wet room. There is no separate shower cubicle. You wash your body and hair sat on a small stool using the shower attachment. Once you are clean and unsoapy, you get into the bath and soak. The idea of washing in the bath is clearly disgusting – you are just soaking in your own dead skin and mess. This way of doing things developed from the public baths that predate in-house plumbing by a few thousand years. If you get in the water dirty, all you are doing is exposing others to your filth. People who visit *onsen* (hot spring public baths) in Japan are warned about the strict and confusing rules, and posters are often displayed making it clear what to do. In reality it's simple, as long as you keep one concept in mind – other people have to use the same bath, so don't put anything that isn't a perfectly clean body into the water. No suds, no flannels, no towels, nothing. You wouldn't want to soak in someone else's epidermis and pubes, so give others the same courtesy.

So we had to destroy the bathroom, rip up the floor, let everything dry out, replace some of the foundation posts of the house, order and install a new bathroom, and, of course, pay for the whole fucking thing.

We tell the *fudō-san*, who it turns out is spoiling for a fight.

'I knew there was something dodgy going on. The estate agent the previous owners employed, I never trusted her.'

'So what can we do?'

'We sue the fuck out of them.'

'Seriously?'

'Sure, they signed a contract stating there were no problems with the building. They must have known about this. So we sue them.'

One problem. In Japan, even if you win a lawsuit, you won't be awarded costs. Whether we won or not, we'd have had to pay the lawyer's fees and there was no guarantee any payout would even cover the cost of the work and the fees. We debated it: the desire for revenge and money weighed against the risk of being even more out of pocket. In the end we reached a compromise.

'We threaten to sue them. That should scare them enough to settle.'

'What if they call our bluff?'

'They won't, they know foreigners love to sue.'

'That's Americans.'

'They don't know that.'

We didn't sue. The threat was enough for them to offer to settle. Kingo called in some friends, some favours, got some materials at cost, but it was still a bill in the millions of yen and it meant we had to use the showers of family and friends or visit an *onsen* every day. (An aside on currency: I will never get used to calculating things in millions. My car cost two million. My house cost twenty-five million. A few years ago I applied for a writer-in-residence position at a university in the US. Under 'previous salary' I wrote 'six million' and accidentally omitted the currency, a mistake I have never made with the student loans people.)

The first time I ever experienced an *onsen* was with my father-in-law and Kingo's eldest son, Haru, who was seven at the time. We were camping at Kawaguchiko, in Yamanashi Prefecture, a lake at the base of Mount Fuji, Minori, her parents, Haru and me. Campsites in Japan rarely have their own shower blocks but are usually near an *onsen* or *sento* (technically, *onsen* are public baths of naturally hot mineral water rising from deep underground and *sento* are public baths of artificially heated water). At the end of the first day we set off in the car to get washed.

'Iain, do you know the rules of the *onsen*?' said Yoji.

'Some of them. Wash before getting in the water. Take a hand towel. Don't put the towel in the water.'

'Yep. Also, you must be naked,' said Miyoko.

'Sure. Hence the hand towel. For modesty.'

'I heard foreigners don't like being naked in public.'

'It depends what you mean by public. I mean, after sports at school there are communal showers, but getting naked during the game is frowned upon.'

'Will you be okay?'

'Sure.'

Because why not? Nudity is the great leveller. You can't be all high and mighty with your folds and wrinkles and blemishes on display. No one can be taken seriously while their flaccid penis floats around, buffeted by ripples and eddies. I have no problem with nudity. I just didn't take into account two facts: I was with the father of my girl-friend, a man I'd only met a handful of times, and a seven-year-old boy who possessed the sense of humour of a seven-year-old boy.

I derobed, threw everything into the locker, grabbed my hand towel and held it strategically over the naughty bits. Too late.

'Iain's penis! Iain's penis! I saw Iain's penis!'

My future father-in-law and I made eye contact, both naked, as Haru danced around at the hilarity of it all. We maintained eye contact, neither of us sure where else to look. I thought back to the times when I'd met the fathers of girls I was dating. All were awkward. All best forgotten. None was ever as awkward or as painfully unforgettable as this. I think perhaps that day was the final coffin nail for my shyness. Once you've been tackle-out with the father of the woman you are having sex with, everything else is a fucking doddle.

I Need All the Friends I Can Get

Loneliness is the expectation of the immigrant. You leave behind everything you know and start again from scratch, everything unfamiliar, everyone a stranger. I arrived in Japan functionally illiterate, unable to speak more than the handful of words I memorised on the plane, not knowing a single person who had even been to Japan on holiday, let alone had lived there. I was setting forth on my own, off into the unknown with no one to rely on but myself.

I didn't take it well at first. I never got homesick, not in the traditional sense of missing my home. I never yearned for Aberdeen or thought about heading to the airport, but I did get so very lonely.

Inuyama is a small commuter town outside Nagoya. No other Nova teachers lived there and I had the two-bedroom apartment to myself. We were given five days to acclimatise before our training began. Everyone else, people who later became my friends, had flatmates, other teachers in the same building. I had no one. All this input, all these new experiences and no one to share it with. It didn't take me long to start cracking up.

I arrived late on the Thursday night, had a couple of cans from the convenience store and fancied a few more social beers. I'd spotted a branch of the school I'd be working for near the station so wandered over there.

An Australian woman and a Japanese woman were behind the desk. 'Hi, can I help you?'

'Yes, I'm new here. I work for Nova and live here now. I just arrived today. I was wondering if anyone fancied grabbing a drink when you get off?'

'Not me, I've got plans, but I'll ask the others.' She disappeared into the staff room for a moment. Reappeared. 'Nope, sorry.'

'Oh, right.'

'Bye, then.'

'Yeah, thanks.'

The next day my luggage arrived (the company had arranged for it to get sent rather than have us lug it around) so I spent the morning turning the contents of one suitcase into my new life, found a supermarket, looked in bafflement at the labels and pictures, got some vegetables (easy to work out what they are), some rice (holy shit, the price! Protectionist taxes mean Japanese rice grown in Japan and sold in Japanese shops is more expensive than Vietnamese rice shipped to Scotland and sold in Tesco – an indictment of protectionism or an indictment of supermarket chains? Sure, why can't it be both?) and a few random things in tins that were less hit and more miss. After dinner the silence started getting to me. I needed company, conversation, alcohol, so I decided to hit the town and try again.

By the station there is a narrow side street with lights and sandwich-board signs. Five businesses in a row. Really bad singing comes from the first four so I gird myself, take a deep breath and slide back the door to the fifth. Taa-daa! The world's smallest bar. It fits seven, sitting along the counter. There are four there already and an elderly woman behind the counter. It's like a western. The piano stops, the record scratches as the door reveals a slightly terrified foreigner. I sit on one of the stools and try my first Japanese sentence. *Biru o kudasai*. She rattles off something I don't understand. Great. After a few gestures I end up with a bottle of Kirin and a glass. The woman in charge tries to talk in broken English, as does the young woman next to me. Ah, Nova! Ah, Scotland! Princess Diana, yes?

She pours my first glass, confirming one rule of etiquette in the *Lonely Planet* – in Japan you don't pour your own beer, you hold your glass while someone else pours. My glass holds a mouthful. I drink it. And wait. And wait. The woman next to me notices and pours. Gone. I wait. I look around me. Everyone else is pouring their own beer. Should I trust the *Lonely Planet* or should I follow the crowd? Bow to peer pressure, always.

A 'Norm!'-type cheer as the door slides back and a young guy, about thirty, comes in. He turns out to be Ken, whose mother is an English teacher.

'You work for Nova? Good luck!'

He translates their questions and my responses, then vice versa.

One man keeps asking about whisky. 'You drink it straight, yes?'

'Yes.'

'It's strong, yes? Thirty per cent, yes?'

'Stronger.'

'No, not possible. Have you tried saké?'

There follows a big discussion about what I should be given. In the end they decide I should have something brewed from sweet potatoes. 'Not strong, not sweet, very nice.' Not strong, my arse, the stuff's like lighter fluid, but tasty lighter fluid. I am then presented with some pork and lettuce, followed by a slice of melon: 'a present. You come back and teach English.'

'If you teach me Japanese.'

'Okay, deal.'

The owner begins talking rapidly and pointing at the clock.

'You have time?' Ken asks.

'Sure.'

'She says I should take you to a bar.'

'This isn't a bar?'

Ken and I head off, to be followed by Ayaka and her husband. 'He trucker. Not very romantic. But he no speak English.' I'm not sure if that's a non sequitur or not.

Just past the street I live on, we come to a small red bar blaring Guns N' Roses and covered in comic book art and featuring a massive tattooed barman who speaks English. This is Kei; born in Yugoslavia (as it was then) to a Japanese mother, he lived for a few years in St Andrews. Small world. Fantastic. I think I have a local.

We get tore into a few more beers, they have some more food. Ken tells me that the bar I met them in is the best bar in town, where everyone is friendly and where visiting professors are taken by the university. First night and I picked it by random: result. I later learn there is no university.

Eventually I saunter home, extremely worse for wear but having had a cracking second night in Japan.

Thirteen years on, my life still exists in the tension between desiring solitude and needing interaction. I want to be alone but loneliness drives me mad. I mentioned that Kerouac's *Desolation Angels* had a big impact on me as a kid. The older I get, the more I realise how much we have in common, and I wonder if it's conditioning or genetic. Did I get entranced by ideas of the solitary poet living a hard life in the mountains because of some combination of genetic bases or because *Dharma Bums*, *Zen and the Art of Motorcycle Maintenance* and *The Glass Bead Game* lay temptingly around the house?

Desolation Angels attracted and terrified me in equal measure. In the book, Jack Duluoz – a renamed Jack Kerouac (there's a PhD thesis in the idea that Kerouac's novels are inspired by the Japanese I-novel, if anyone can be bothered) – takes a job as a fire lookout in the mountains of the Pacific Northwest. He is alone for weeks in a cabin high in the peaks keeping an eye out for forest fires, drinking wine, meditating, worrying about bears and going slightly mad. As I read and imagined myself into Jack's world a dread began to take me over. How would I cope? I'd arrive with my wine, my notebooks and pens, all good intentions and romantic ideas of poetry and nature, of muses and inner voices. How long would it take me to crack up? What would cause it?

The reason that girl on my school trip to France preferred me silent is that once I pop, I can't stop. My introversion wasn't because I wished to be away from others, it was because I had no idea how to interact with the rest of my species. I have a huge propensity for saying the wrong thing, for putting my foot up to the hip in my mouth, for being totally unable to read a room, and am ill-equipped to deal with my fuck-ups. Once I felt I was on solid ground, a desperate need to speak, to be heard, to be understood took over. I'm convinced this is why I am so attracted to writing: I can speak to others from a safe distance. I can formulate exactly what I want to say and be miles away when it reaches you. I need to run, to put distance between myself and the rest of humanity, but I can't stand to be away from you all. I'm like an addict. I guess that's what drew me to ascetics, Zen monks who would self-mummify, hermits in caves and grizzly men up mountains. They'd broken that attachment, defeated the desire that leads to suffering, learned to exist outside the dialectic of humanity. Oh, how I envy them.

Going full Kerouac scared me. Instead I moved 5,000 miles from home, but to a densely populated developed country. Then I moved away from the densely populated area but made sure I still had neighbours, that I was twenty-five minutes from a highway interchange, twenty minutes from a supermarket, ten from a train station. We looked at a house in Nagano, in the hills, down a two-mile dirt track, beyond the rice fields and outside the metal fences to keep bears at bay. It was gorgeous, everything I claimed I wanted. It made me feel like *Desolation Angels* did. That terror. To be alone but not alone, that's the tension, the line I try to balance on.

What does it mean to be accepted into a community? Does it mean you hang out with your neighbours every day, swap sugar and stories, run in and out of each other's houses? Or does it mean they leave you alone to get on with your life while they get on with theirs? And which did I want?

I've seen examples of both. My aunt and uncle had a close relationship with their neighbours – kids the same age, shared interests, more like extended family than neighbours. Minori's parents never speak to their neighbours; not in a cold way, just because everyone's getting on with their own things and none of the circles in the Venn diagram of life cross. Others I know have active running battles with their neighbours. I definitely didn't want that model.

Minori is very much in the second camp. Civil, but not overly friendly. On speaking terms, but no confidences shared. I wavered between the two. I enjoyed drinking with Kensuke, was curious about his time at art school, the beaten VW camper van he still had from those days when he'd driven around Japan. But after those initial months it became clear that the second form of relationship was inevitable.

It's an old adage that as the years go by, it becomes harder to make friends. It's certainly harder to make close friends, but age isn't the obstacle. Kids are.

We don't have any and we're not going to. We thought about it for a while, weighed options, pros and cons, did a few practice runs, but ultimately decided that while kids are fine, holidays are better. I've justified our decision in different ways to different people – because some people still demand a justification for what is essentially none of their fucking business, can't cope with the idea that someone might make a different decision and have different priorities from them. But in truth, and as always with me, it comes back to something I read. In *Farewell Waltz* by Milan Kundera, Jakub is explaining to Bertlef his reasons for eschewing the biological imperative. His argument culminates in the following exchange:

> 'Having a child is to show an absolute accord with mankind. If I have a child, it's as though I'm saying: I was born and have tasted life and declare it so good that it merits being duplicated.'
>
> 'And you have not found life to be good?' asked Bertlef.
>
> Jakub tried to be precise, and said cautiously: 'All I know is that I could never say with complete conviction: Man is a wonderful being and I want to reproduce him.'

The human race will continue just fine without Minori and I adding one more mouth to it. We're fine with that. It's just that it seems to baffle others. They react like our choosing not to have children is an indictment of their choices. It isn't. The fact that you choose the spaghetti while I opt for the pizza doesn't mean I am judging you and your pasta-loving ilk, it just means that my taste runs this way and yours that, and that's an end to it.

Back in Scotland, many of my friends and peers are making similar choices. Some are married and child-free. Others have children with long-term partners but aren't married. Others have children and no partners. Some are divorced, remarried, single and proud of it; some embraced marriage when the law changed and they were allowed to do so; others welcomed the change in law in theory but felt it didn't change how they lived their lives. Amongst my friends and peers, people just do as they wish and only the narrow- and feeble-minded give a damn. In Japan, things haven't progressed that far. A friend's mother is freaking out because he is twenty-seven and not married. Another friend reached thirty, married the first woman who came along – also thirty and panicking – and was divorced two years later. I was once asked by a Japanese guy during a drinking party if I had kids. I said no, and he laughed and called me *sukebe*, which literally translates as 'lewd' or 'pervert' or something similar. The other Japanese guys couldn't follow his logic either and he wouldn't explain himself, but clearly he thought there was something weird about a man getting married and not having kids, like maybe I was a swinger or something like that.

My peers in Japan, they are all about their kids. That's life, that's what you do. Get married, have kids, the man works, the woman cooks, the kids are the centre of the world. They are also the particles that bond, the atoms that combine to form complex molecules. There's a Japanese compound word, *mama-tomo*, mother-friend, meaning mothers who are friends because their kids are friends, in the same class or after-school club. Kids, in Japan, are the passport to friendship. Without kids, your lives and interests are incompatible. Kensuke has three kids. I have none. From his point of view, in the world he lives in, he and I have nothing in common. From the start, we're destined to be neighbours, not friends. It's inevitable that after the novelty of being the only *gaijin* in the village wears off, everyone will get on with their lives and, assuming we've been accepted, they'll leave us to get on with ours.

I've always existed within that tension between solitude and interaction. This is how I know I've found my place, my home: I'm close enough to keep the terror at bay, far enough to breathe free. There are more rural places in Japan than this, but were I there, how long would it take for me to crack up? I need to know there is community, but I need to be on the fringe. That's my place, my comfort zone. It's the tension that holds me together.

Kei is from Sarajevo, and got out when the war started. Through his mother he got a Japanese passport but before settling here he lived in Scotland. I only got to the bottom of how he ended up studying English in St Andrews a year after I met him, when my dad first came out to visit. My father spent his career in the fire brigade. One of his colleagues, Ronnie, volunteered to drive a bus to Belgrade and back, helping refugees get out as the country fell apart. Kei was on his bus. After a couple of months in London he moved to St Andrews where they offered language courses for refugees. Small world. All it needed was Kevin Bacon clinging to the chassis to make it smaller.

Strange, isn't it, to think back to a time when Britain sent buses across Europe to save people from war? Today the buses would be filled going the other way, Britain's apparent belief in fairness and the underdog spirit only valid if Britain is being treated unfairly or the underdog is white.

Kei's bar became my home from home in those first lonely months, and I'd never have survived the solitude if it hadn't been for him and his family. I drank there, ate there, learned my first Japanese words there, made friends, learned how to count in Japanese by playing darts. I even worked behind the bar on Hogmanay and the mezzanine hosted the one and only gig of the band I started with Thom, Welcome Camel.

*

There's an intensity to those early friendships. We were all around twenty-four, a long way from home, all experiencing this new culture, new life, for the first time together. Scots, English, Aussies, Kiwis, Americans, different socio-economic, ethnic, political backgrounds, bonded by the same need for community, for comfort in numbers, the need to stave off the loneliness. Francis and I were on the same flight to Japan from Heathrow in 2005. He and Thom were in the same apartment building. In 2012 we were co-best men at Thom's wedding, and as I write this there's an ongoing WhatsApp conversation to plan a weekend of silliness in Dublin. Friendship forged on the fringes of solitude goes deep, lasts long.

In the last year, both of my mother's parents have died, my last surviving grandparents. They were both in their nineties, enjoyed long, fulfilling lives. I wrote obliquely about my grandfather, about their generation, in my first novel *First Time Solo*. Doing that book made me closer to both of them, the conversations we had, digging into their youth, the daily stuff that doesn't make up the usual anecdotes, the brands of cigarettes, the songs they danced to, the practical jokes played and the things that kept them awake at night. When I left for Japan, my grandmother said, 'If we die, don't come back. We won't mind; we won't be here.' It was a sweet, honest thing to say but it also gave me pause. At that point I was only thinking a year ahead at the most, a few months in reality. I had no intention of staying in Japan for ever, but maybe she sensed something, or maybe it was just her inbuilt pessimism about her chances of survival.

My grandma died first, fighting to the last, desperate to survive. My granddad followed a few months later, unable or unwilling to live without her. Each time I lit a fire in my garden, I'd sit there all day remembering. They would have loved my house in Gifu. They lived in a small village in Aberdeenshire, their house once the home of the gardener for the nearby estate. Big gardens, tall trees, organisation and chaos side by side. I spent my childhood in those trees.

Trees are comforting. Trees are home. These falling autumn leaves reconnect me with my childhood, with my grandparents, my family, with home. Maybe I wouldn't have felt so alone in Kerouac's mountains after all.

Rockin' the Suburbs

Most writers are failed rock stars – I know I am. The Venn diagram of authors and poets who are also in bands is so overlapping as to look like sloppy superimposition. I'm not sure what the drive is – the desire for something more collaborative, the need for instant feedback in the form of applause and dancing, or simply an overspill of creativity pushing us into different art forms, the two pursuits seeming to complement each other well.

My first compositions were songs. The lyrics morphed into poetry once I reached puberty – my voice didn't so much break as shatter – and eventually narrative and character took over and prose became my playground. But music stayed with me. I was in a band in high school, another one after university (for some reason hindsight hasn't elucidated, I turned away from music at university, the very time I could have been most enthusiastic) and the urge returned in Japan.

Thom and I, single and possessed with enough facial hair to competently handle two acoustic guitars, formed the legendary Welcome Camel in early 2006.

The name derives from a piece of bullshit. Few people in Japan know anything about Scotland. One of the Japanese women who worked in my school knew less than nothing and it occasionally amused me to tell her exaggerated fibs. It started with the standard haggis story (one leg shorter than the other) and peaked with the Welcome Camel. The story went like this . . .

Japan has welcome cats, those waving cat statues businesses put in the window to entice customers. If the left paw is waving, it is supposed to draw in customers. If it's the right paw, it attracts money. Since presumably the customers have money, and money can't come in without being carried by a customer, it really doesn't matter which paw is waving, but we live in an age of choice, so choices we have. Kyoko asked me if we have something similar in Scotland. I told her that our sacred animal was the camel, a majestic creature that once roamed the Scottish hills and glens but which was hunted to extinction. Scots today believe that a few survive in secret pockets of the Highlands and that to see one is incredibly lucky, so businesses put waving camels in the windows of establishments. Her credulity became immortalised as our band name.

Kei offered us a gig, using the mezzanine/tattoo parlour part of the shop as a stage. Over a few weeks we practised a bunch of covers and wrote three originals ('Home' and 'You Should Go If You've Never Been' by me and 'The Horse You Rode In On' by Thom). The gig was set for 25 March, a Tuesday night. Thom invaded Inuyama the night before armed with his guitar and a set list. My blog at the time suggests it was this:

Bluebell Morning (Ooberman)

Home

. . . And The Horse You Rode In On

Good Riddance (Time Of Your Life) (Green Day)

Instrumental

Get Me Away From Here (I'm Dying) (Belle and Sebastian)

Take Me Out (Iain's version) (Franz Ferdinand)

Instrumental (mine)

Where Is My Mind? (Pixies)

You Should Go If You've Never Been (Mine)

But I have no memory of playing 'Take Me Out' nor what the second instrumental could have been. Another note I have says that we at least practised 'Californication' by the Red Hot Chili Peppers, but as I've never learned to play more than the introduction to that, there's no way that's true. Perhaps, like all great pre-internet milestones in rock history, it is lost for ever to the mists of mythology and hagiography.

Kei lent us the keys to the bar so we set up at about 11.30 a.m. and had a practice. So far, so good. Had a break, some coffee. Had another practice. Not so good this time. Thom was shaky on some of the words, my G-string kept slipping (ooh, vicar). Had a break. Had another run through, this one much better but decided to drop the Pixies song as it sounded pathetic. Kei arrived about six and we arsed around from then until nine playing darts, taking photos, eating dinner and trying not to think about our impending debut. An audience of twelve, which is what Jesus usually played to. We climbed the rickety steps to the tattoo parlour, got on our stools, guitared up, and I played the intro to 'Bluebell Morning'. Nothing. Looked at Thom. Started again. He got the first line out, forgot the second line, froze completely and we had to start again, again.

We got through the set okay, lots of mistakes, some songs received better than others. But generally the opinion was one of success. No one seemed to expect a huge amount anyway and we were pleasantly surprised, which I find is the safest way to approach life.

After the gig we were feeling a bit deflated but we got stuck straight into the beer and whisky, and slowly Thom and I relaxed. After about an hour, people requested an encore, so we went up, played a few more songs, this time karaoke with the audience. I remember we did play the Chili Peppers this time, some more Green Day, Smashing Pumpkins, stuff like that. Someone taught me to play an Arcade Fire song, but who it was and which song is lost in time. A few folk drifted away for the last train but the majority who had Wednesday off work stayed over. Next day was the Tagata Jinja Penis Festival, and no one wanted to miss that.

It didn't take long for John to suggest drinking games. First we introduced 'International Drinking Rules', which just about did for Mitchell. He was drinking punishment Zima at such a rate that Kei had bottles already opened behind the bar so he could just hand him one. By this point the whisky had set into Thom and he was wandering about in a daze and playing darts by himself. John and Mitchell got into the age-old UK versus Australia fight, set off by the classic joke: what's the difference between Australia and a yoghurt? If you leave a yoghurt out in the sun, it develops a culture. I have to say that Mitchell won in the end, with this beautiful piece of logic.

John: We discovered you.

Mitchell: You discovered me?

John: Yes.

Mitchell: How could you discover me when I was already part of you when you discovered me?

Two weeks later I called Thom up and asked about our next gig.

'I have a girlfriend now. I don't need to be in a band.'

Welcome Camel never played again, slipping into rock and roll lore. Another great band broken up by a woman. An English woman in Japan. A Japanese woman in England. History repeats.

In the 'Nuclear Holiday' chapter, I wrote about redecorating the *tatami* room. It's actually two rooms, the entire northern end of the house – the bad end if you believe in feng shui, traditional Japanese architecture and *Game of Thrones* – separated by *shōji* (sliding doors). After painting I took out the separating doors and removed the paper from those covering the patio doors at either end. What had been a cold, dark room was transformed into a large, warm, spacious and welcoming place.

Minori and I like to collect art, particularly from places we've travelled to, and this room has become home to figurines from Vietnam, oil paintings from South Korea, pencil sketches from Singapore and abstract work done directly on driftwood from Thailand. The cupboards are also full of cute plastic and paper bags, baroquely designed boxes and interesting wrapping paper Minori has picked up along the way, but they remain hidden from sight, forgotten but kept, like an appendix or Gibraltar. My favourite artwork is a series of pastel drawings by an artist from Myanmar we met in Bangkok, scenes from traditional rural life there that for some reason remind me of adventure books I read as a child. The room has an eclectic, artistic flavour, the idea being that eventually, when we redesign the kitchen and dining room, this will become the living room. A big sofa, a projector and screen, under-floor heating. The whole bit.

At least, that's what I told Minori.

Actually, it's my studio.

There are no windows apart from the two patio doors at either end – it's bad luck to put windows on the north gable. That side of the house is pointed away from the neighbours. It's a room that Minori tends not to use much beyond launching her coats into upon returning home or for storing the free-standing pull-up bar she uses to train for bouldering. It's where I strategically stored my guitars when we moved in. Strategically. Temporarily. Yeah, right.

Aside: I always loved the story of the lecturer telling her class that while two negatives can make a positive, two positives can never make a negative. One student pipes up from the back, 'Yeah, right.' I think I like it not just for the word play but because I like anything that bursts the bubble of motivational nonsense. Our office at work (there are eight of us, battery-farmed in cubicles) is covered in such cynical, bubble-bursting quotes. There is a certain type of person who finds greater motivation in cynicism than in positivity. I am whole-cold-heartedly in that camp.

Like pioneer species, the guitars colonised and spread. When my dad visited in that first October, he and my stepmother Catherine strolled through customs at Central Japan International Airport with the love of my life in tow, my precious, my darling turquoise blue Fender Jag-Stang with the chip out of the third fret, the whammy bar that falls out if you attempt to pogo and the R&B Music Aberdeen strap I've had since my eighteenth birthday.

That was all the impetus I needed. I went to Hard Off – yes, Hard Off, a chain of second-hand electrical stores – and bought an amp, a bunch of pedals, cables, picks and strings. There is also Book Off for second-hand books, CDs and DVDs, House Off for furniture and furnishings, and, I swear to God, a shop in Osu, in Nagoya, that sells alcohol called Liquor Off. There's a Liquor Off in Osu in Nagoya – go, take a selfie there, everyone else does. I set to work relearning scales and songs. I turned the amp up, stationed Minori in the garden, and blasted out the riff from Pearl Jam's 'Spin The Black Circle'.

'Can you hear anything?'

'What?'

'Very funny. Was it too loud?'

'No, I can't hear anything.'

And with that, Minori lost any chance of a new living room.

Indifference

Some of us immigrants in Japan get awfully het up about fitting in. There are certain foreigner-in-Japan tropes that arise again and again in conversation, in blogs, in my-year-in-Japan memoirs. They all revolve around a similar central point, a series of micro-aggressions that underlines our status as outsiders. They are clichés, based in fact, but unoriginal hobby horses. They are the reason it's taken me thirteen years to consider writing my own year-in-Japan memoir. As a critic for the *Japan Times* newspaper I've railed against many of these stories, the repetitive blandness of the chopsticks, kimonos and kanji tales. Plentiful are the stories of 'welcome to Japan, when are you going home?'. Bountiful are the anecdotes about how 'you can use chopsticks, aren't you talented?' and 'your Japanese is so good!' when all you've said is thank you. Yes, these things happen, and yes, they are annoying, but so fucking what. Life is annoying. People are annoying. It's not like life was perfect wherever we came from. We wouldn't have left if it was. These irritations happened back home as well, just with different details.

The classic is the empty seat trope. All immigrants in Japan have had the experience of finding the seat next to them on the train remaining empty in the overcrowded carriage. It's taken by some as proof of a tacit racism – they'd rather stand, squashed together for the forty-five-minute commute, than sit next to a foreigner. And no doubt some people do make that calculation; arseholes are everywhere. But the people I've seen complain most vociferously about this highlighting of their outsider status, about the Japanese refusal to treat them the same as they would a Japanese person, are usually the ones who, like me, don't fit snugly into a single seat on a Japanese train. The spaces are narrow. I have broad shoulders. I spill over on to the next seat. I wouldn't try to squeeze in next to me either. I have found, by experimentation, that when I make myself narrower – pull my shoulders forward while I read my book, for example – the seat miraculously fills up. School children have no problem sitting next to me. An elderly woman the other day chose the seat next to me over the Japanese bloke manspreading opposite. Sure, there are racists here, and sure, we'll never really fit in – I won't, all six foot one, white and blond of me – but it's not always because of race. No one wants to sit next to the loud, obnoxious person talking on their phone, regardless of where they were born. No one wants some random guy's thigh pressing against them, regardless of his skin colour.

Besides, what's the obsession with fitting in? Being different isn't a curse. Being discriminated against for being different is a problem, so much so that it has been made a crime in many countries. But feeling hard done by because my neighbours treat me differently than they treat someone who has spent all their life in the village is just stupid. I get treated differently because they don't know me. I'm new, I'm an unknown quantity. They also treat my wife differently from the other wives, because she's an incomer as well. At the first New Year meeting, I met a man who, with his family, had moved into the area ten months before we did. Our experiences turned out to be pretty similar, except that he'd been roped into doing a lot more volunteering than I had, and that was purely because of his skills. He had experience as a volunteer fireman and they needed someone to look after health and safety issues for the community – extinguishers and alarms in the meeting hall, potential fire hazards if there were a dry summer – things I'd be useless at. Of course they hadn't asked me. They'd asked him and he'd had no choice but to say yes. Being treated differently isn't always a bad thing.

In Scotland I felt alienated. I never felt comfortable, never felt at home. The alienation ground me down because there was no reason I could think of why I should feel that way – whether I really was alienated or not. Here, of course, I'm alienated! I'm an alien! I feel so much more at home, so much less alienated here than in my own country because at least here my alienation makes sense. I have that photo, taken by Francis, of me standing at a crosswalk in Nagoya, waiting to cross. There's about 200 Japanese people, roughly the same height, all black hair. And me, blond and tall, a head above the rest. Photographic proof that I am different, that I stick out. Why fight that? Why deny that I am different? Difference isn't bad, at least not to the vast majority of people. Arseholes are arseholes everywhere. Who cares what they think?

Too Raging to Cheers

Let's get this straight from the start. The Kirin Cup isn't a cup. It isn't even a tournament. It's a marketing exercise by the Kirin beer company. Two international football teams are invited to Japan for a round-robin with the winner awarded the Kirin Cup. It isn't a real trophy, it isn't a real tournament. But in our 148-year history (the first international football game was Scotland v. England in 1872, a 0–0 draw) it is the only tournament we have ever won, the only trophy in our cabinet, and in the last twenty-two years, the only tournament we've even been in, so we're claiming it. It's ours. Scotland, Kirin Cup winners, 2006.

I was in Japan then, and watched it on TV, the distance to Saitama being a bit beyond my budget at the time. Scotland, in an echo of that first ever match, ground out a boring scoreless draw but after beating Bulgaria 5–1, it was enough. So when Scotland returned in 2009 for the even-less-like-a-real-tournament Kirin Challenge Cup (literally a one-off friendly with the fallacy of a trophy at the end dangled like a limp carrot in front of an apathetic donkey), I wasn't going to miss out on the glory.

It's like the in-laws meeting. Japan versus Scotland. A friendly.

The Nissan Stadium, Yokohama, site of the 2002 World Cup Final. We travel through to Yokohama and check in, ten minutes from the stadium. Far enough to enjoy the crowds on the approach, close enough to escape. We get dressed up; it's a special occasion after all. Minori's in a Scotland top, with a Japanese flag around her shoulders. On the way in, we stop at a face-painting stand and each get a *hinomaru* – the Japanese rising sun – painted on one cheek, a saltire on the other. I'm sporting Shunsuke Nakamura's number 10 top from the 2006 World Cup and an enormous saltire tied round my waist, hanging like a Highland sarong, and a Lion Rampant cape, flying in the wind like Marvel's William Wallace. We look good, an advert for multiculturalism.

On the way out of the hotel we take the lift with some Japanese guys.

'Scotland?'

'*Hai.*'

'You don't wear skirt?'

'No.'

'*Nande?*'

'I forgot to shave my legs.'

Beers, photos, cheers and chants. We bought our tickets in the country so we're in amongst the Japanese fans, main stand, far from the tiny pocket of Tartan Army, a little village of indomitable Gaels in the corner. In Japan there's only a vague attempt at fan segregation because there's no violence, no atmosphere of threat. Football is a family day out; you bring the wife and kids, your packed lunch and your noise-makers. Saying that, they're getting cannier with foreign fans. I was at the FIFA Club World Cup at Toyota Stadium in 2011, an infamous game amongst those who were there. The authorities were in no way prepared for the Espérance de Tunis fans, fresh from ousting Ben Ali earlier in the Arab Spring. They were rowdy, they were dancing, they were singing, they were drinking. They would not take their seats and they were in no way intimidated by the teenage ball boys deployed to stop a pitch invasion when dodgy refereeing handed Al Sadd of Qatar a 2–1 win. It was hilarious, by far the most fun I've ever had at a sports event. The following year, there were fences and guards and much less fun.

Back in Yokohama, the teams come out, line up, and it's anthem time. The Japanese one, sad, interminable, slowly fades into life and people start singing mournfully. I maintain this anthem is to blame for much underperforming by Japanese teams. An anthem should be rous-ing, bordering on martial, certainly in a major key, and ideally with a bit of bombast, something to get the blood flowing, the adrenaline pumping, something, well, anthemic. What it shouldn't be is a dirge that would make Radiohead go 'fucking hell, cheer up, mate'. Still, everyone sings along. A round of applause. Then it's our turn, 'Flower Of Scotland'. That's more like it. Rousing, bloody, even has gaps perfectly suited to a gloss of swearing. I feel a bit self-conscious, the only one in the main stand giving it laldy, but you've got to represent, and it really is a very rousing anthem.

They start to boo. The people around me. And with each boo I sing a little louder. And a little louder. Then I stand up, flag up. Alone. I can barely hear the fifty outriders of the Tartan Army at the other end, but the indignation, the anger, makes me add my voice to theirs. I try to drown out the booing. I fail.

I sit down in a purple rage, fists clenched.

'Good job,' says the man two seats along. 'Good singing.'

'Fuck you,' I say. 'Fuck you. Why did you boo?'

'Boo?'

I show him.

'To show we support Japan.'

'You hate Scotland?'

'No.'

'To boo means you hate something. You all said, "I hate Scotland. Scotland can fuck off." Well, you can fuck off, too.'

He says nothing, looks at the pitch.

'Cunt.'

Minori breaks her silence. 'Leave it.'

A drubbing. 2–0. Should have been more. None of the regular first team have travelled, Japan is at full strength. Honda scores both. Smirks around me. I'm not singing any more. Scotland isn't well known in Japan. Now they know something about us. They know we're crap at football. My students are going to rip the piss when I get back to work. We leave. The crowds mix, and the kids are fascinated by these massive guys in skirts. Up ahead one is teaching them English.

'Say fuck.'

'FAKU.'

'No, not FAKU, Fuck. Fuck.'

'FAKU. FAKU.'

'Better. Not great. Now. The.'

'ZA.'

'Not za, the. The.' And he makes this sound like a snake with a lisp.

'Thrpp,' the kids say, blowing raspberries.

'Together. Fuck the.'

'FAKUZA.'

'Pope.'

His mates are in stitches. A father says to me, in Japanese, 'What's he teaching them?'

'A football chant.'

'Is it bad?'

'It's not good.'

He looks like he wants to intervene, to say something.

I shake my head. 'Leave it.'

Is this how they see me? They're like the goons in the Popeye cartoons. Huge slabs of flesh, knuckles hanging low. 'Hey, pal, vodka Coke, eh.' We've gone into a bar for some food and drink, see what the craic is.

'Vodka fuckin' Coke, *capisce*?'

'Fucksake, this is Bacardi, no fuckin' vodka. Hey, pal, Ah said vodka. V-O-D-K-A. Understand?'

I intervene.

'Wokka cora?'

'Wokka nai.' Cocktail bars have vodka, but not a regular place like this. No one drinks vodka Coke here. I translate. The kind of attitude that would vote for Brexit rises, outraged that what you can get in Barrhead you can't automatically get in Yokohama.

'Come on, let's get out of here. We'll go to an *izakaya*. There won't be any fans there.'

As Minori finishes her drink I go up to pay. There's fear, exhaustion, something in the guy's eyes as he watches me approach. What hassle am

I going to give him? Relief when I ask for the bill in Japanese, hand over the money without any problems. As he gives me my change, I say, '*Gomenne. Konya, ganbarre.*' Sorry about this. Good luck tonight.

He grabs my hand and starts shaking it. '*Arigatō.* Thank you. Good night.'

We go home.

Line of Best Fit

Assimilation is something that is often portrayed as a sudden and violent act. A complete upheaval of character, a total negation of the individual: the Roman Empire, the Borg, Rangers Football Club. There's a line you cross and you become something different, something worse. Resistance is futile.

It's not really like that. First, assimilation isn't always bad. It's another way of looking at multiculturalism, for example: two previously separate groups become entwined, both changing in positive ways while retaining something of the original. It's the European ideal, harmony in distinctiveness. Another word for assimilation is acclimatisation.

For the immigrant, there is no line, no binary switch, no zero-sum game. The only way to know you've changed is to measure yourself against where you came from. To your new community, especially in rural Japan, you'll always be other, never quite be the right size of peg for that hole. To them, you'll always be the person from over there. But to the people from over there, you become something new. I measure my assimilation against visitors, and the clearest examples are family.

One famous question foreigners are asked by Japanese people inexperienced in being around foreigners is: 'Why don't people in your country take their shoes off when they go into their house?' There's no point trying to bring nuance into any *answer* to this question – 'my family do' or 'some cultures do' will be met by blank stares. The popular assumption is that all Japanese people take their shoes off, and no one else does. To be honest, before I came to Japan I never really thought about it, but the first time I was asked, I couldn't think of a decent answer. Yes, some people do take their shoes off. But some don't. Watch any British or American film on Netflix right now and there will be scenes of people walking in and out of their homes fully shod. Kids will jump on the sofa in their shoes, teenagers will lie on their beds wearing shoes, and we in the West don't even notice, but Japanese people do. It's not only Marie Kondo who would watch *E.T.* with half a mind on the filth being dragged in from outside. Because that's the end result – houses where people wear their shoes inside are filthy. Think of all the crap on the pavement, on the road, on the corridor at work and down the aisle of the bus or train. You're spreading that all over your carpet and then letting babies crawl around in it.

'Why don't people in your country take their shoes off when they go into their house?'

'Because we don't care all that much about filth.'

I became assimilated. In Japan every house has a *genkan*, a tiled entrance inside the front door where shoes are worn and kept. There is then a step or two up into the house. Japanese people literally invite you to 'step up', not come in. There's a visibly clear line of demarcation. Shoes off here. Socks or slippers from here on in. Visiting friends somehow just don't see this step and forget to take their shoes off. They try on different shoes with their outfits in the bedroom before going out. Or they go the other way. One visitor took their shoes off outside, sitting on the bench in my garden, then walked through the mud in their socks and into the house. I honestly just can't even . . . What thought process leads to that?

That was the moment I realised I'd gone beyond a certain level of assimilation. I could understand, fully, viscerally, for the first time, why so many people asked: 'Why don't people in your country take their shoes off when they go into their house?' Because it's so obviously wrong on a rational, emotional and hygienic level, that's why.

Now the conversation goes:

'Why don't people in your country take their shoes off when they go into their house?'

'I know, right? What the fuck is up with that?'

*

Of course here I'm talking about cultural assimilation, not linguistic. Over the years of living in a country where I have to use my second language but where my day job is teaching people whose second language is my first language, I've done a lot of thinking about measuring progress. There's a famous adage in language teaching in reference to expanding your vocabulary: going from zero to your first hundred words feels like a massive leap. You can recognise the difference, see the progress you've made. The difference between 2,400 words and 2,500 words is too small to notice. After a certain point, progress becomes very hard to gauge. Tests can do it, but you can end up studying only what comes up in the exam without parlaying that into everyday use. I prefer the anecdotal life-goal method, where successfully completing something native speakers take for granted levels you up. For example:

The first time you successfully order a pizza over the phone.

The first time you get a haircut and leave the barber/salon pleased.

The first time you visit a doctor/dentist and aren't terrified.

The first time you successfully get someone to come back to yours.

I still haven't managed all of those. The first time I went for a haircut, about six weeks after moving to Inuyama, was a learning experience. Kyoko, one of the Japanese admin staff at the school phonetically wrote down: *Kaminoke kitte kudasai*. Cut my hair, please. Which was, I thought, very useful as an opener. Which of course it wasn't. I was walking into a barber's shop. What did they think I wanted? A cake? A holiday for two in Guam? My car MOT'd? Of course I wanted a haircut. But what kind of haircut? What did I want them to do to my hair?

And I couldn't answer them, could I? We got as far as 'short' and that was it. I walked out looking like a new Marine recruit, like something about to get yelled at in *Full Metal Jacket*. I kept scaring myself in the mirror and asking myself searching questions about golf balls and garden hoses.

How do you describe a haircut? I mean, even in English I don't have the vocabulary or phrasing to explain what I want beyond 'shorter than it currently is and styled in a way that makes me look like sex on a stick but requires little to no maintenance'.

Now I travel by train for two hours each way every time I need a haircut because that's how far it is to Yoshi's shop, and Yoshi speaks English. We've got to the point where I just ask for 'the usual' and we never refer to my hair again. Perfection.

What does assimilation feel like in the village? I'm not sure. The closest I've come to feeling like I'm belonging was while walking to the station with my friend Steve. We passed Sasaki coming the other way and he stopped to chat. We exchanged a few pleasantries, I introduced Steve, Sasaki nodded and turned back to me. We talked for another five or ten minutes, and in that time he never once more acknowledged Steve's presence. I was known, I was familiar, and he was happy to pass time with me. Steve was something new, an outsider, unfamiliar, how I'd once been to him.

Progress, measurable in increments but only anecdotally.

Without You I'm Nothing

In October my father and stepmother came out to visit. It was the third time he'd been out, the second time for Catherine. The first time they both came together had been when Minori and I got married.

Minori was opposed to a wedding, in the way that gravity is opposed to levitation – it just wasn't happening, no matter how much I wished. I'm an old romantic, and have been known to tear up at other people's weddings (after a lot of drinks, obviously, and in a totally manly way), but Minori is so unromantic she's positively modernist. A wedding was as likely to happen as me discovering that one of my Japanese maples is really a dozing Ent.

Japanese weddings are all ceremony and yet not legally binding. The celebrant has no powers to actually marry people, only the City Office can do that. What tends to happen is people go to the City Office, get the paperwork out the way, and then start planning the wedding. With no wedding to plan, we figured we could get the whole lot out of the way in one day.

'What'll we do after the City Office?'

'Go home. If I can get a night shift before or after, I won't need to take a day off.'

'So after we get married you're going to either go to sleep or go to work?'

'Yeah. Why?'

'No.'

'So what are we going to do? Do I need to use my annual leave?'

'Take the day off. I'll organise everything. You sit over there and look up "romantic" in the dictionary.'

*

On one hand, I was on her side. Japanese weddings are bizarre things. There's the traditional Shinto wedding, a sombre, ritual-filled affair that's becoming increasingly unpopular. I've been to nine weddings in Japan; only one of them has been Shinto and that was Francis and Ayaka's, at Francis's insistence, i.e. the only traditional Japanese wedding I've been to was that of an Englishman.

More popular of late is the Western style, or the mock-Western style. At a guess, this is probably the biggest growth industry in Japan since the bubble burst in the 1990s. It is modelled on the Christian church wedding – white dresses, bouquet throwing and cakes – but with a Japanese twist. Basically, they've done to the Christian wedding what they did to pizzas – they saw one once in a Hollywood film, took a stab at recreating it but very quickly went off in their own unique direction. (A quick look at the Domino's menu tucked behind the Simpsons Aberdeen Fishmonger blackboard hanging in the kitchen – a weird and wonderful housewarming present from Catherine – reveals 'umami-rich salami and fried potato', 'crab and shrimp in white sauce', 'mashed potato and mayonnaise' and, disgustingly, 'ham and pineapple'.)

At these weddings, there are numerous costume changes, a video montage of photos put together by the friends of the bride and groom (hilariously, for me at least, the music accompanying this montage at Minori's brother's wedding was 'Every Breath You Take' by The Police, that classic creepy stalker song) and the interminable speeches. First comes the speech by the groom's boss. Yes, you are expected to invite your boss and colleagues, and your boss is expected to deliver a speech. Fine if you get on with your boss, but if you work for a huge conglomerate – as my friend Kazuki does – and your boss has only a vague idea of who you are, then the speech can be an embarrassing (or hilarious, again, if you're me) mountain of platitudes of the insert-name-here variety. These speeches tend to go on way too long. A note to speechmakers at weddings: you are not addressing the UN. You are rallying troops for the festivities ahead. Guerrilla speechifying is the way to go: get in, make 'em laugh, make 'em cry, get out. Ten minutes max. Fifty minutes isn't a speech, it's a lecture. At Minori's sister's wedding, the boss's speech went on so long I thought Yoji was going to stab him. You see, you're not allowed to start drinking until the last speech has been completed. He and I were sitting at a table loaded down with all the delights Japanese brewing and distilling has to offer, and we weren't allowed a drop until the droning stopped.

Then there's the bride's speech. This Japanese innovation could be ranked as a crime against humanity. Based entirely on the idea that the woman is the property of the father and is now being handed over to a new owner, the bride is expected to make a tearful – literally – speech thanking her parents for raising her and providing for her to date. It is mortifying for all concerned, cloying, humiliating and underpinned by some reprehensible social attitudes. It was this more than anything that made Minori refuse to countenance a wedding. Her parents agreed.

'There's no way you could deliver a speech like that sincerely,' said Miyoko.

'I wouldn't be able to keep a straight face,' said Yoji.

And that was that. No wedding for us.

One last note on Japanese weddings before we move on. The single most amazing aspect of the Japanese mock-Western wedding is the priest.

Yep. The priest.

This is becoming less common, but for a long time the thing that made the wedding most 'traditional' and properly Western was the white guy in robes officiating over it all. Japan has very little history of Christianity beyond enclaves like Nagasaki, and Christians were banned from the country for hundreds of years. Basically the shogun took one look at the mess Spanish and Portuguese Jesuit missionaries had wreaked across the rest of Asia and did the geopolitical equivalent of slamming the door in a Jehovah's Witness's face. Thanks but no thanks. The Dutch fared much better.

'Hi. We'd like to trade with you.'

'Are you Christians?'

'Not so you'd notice.'

'You choose: trade or proselytising.'

'Um . . . trade, please.'

As a result, ideas about Christianity are ceremonial rather than theological. The number of confusing conversations I had about Christian theology when the film of *The Da Vinci Code* came out made me hate the book even more. You try explaining in your second language the Trinity, the Crucifixion and the Resurrection to someone who only wants to understand why Tom Hanks ended up in a chapel in Scotland. As I mentioned before, the actual wedding ceremony in Japan is entirely non-binding. Whoever officiates has zero legal power, so you could just as easily get your cat to do it. But visuals are important and a white guy in robes looks the part. If he has long hair and a Jesus goatee, so much the better.

Celebrant – or fake priest – is a great job, one I've considered doing a couple of times (my atheist core is tickled by the sheer level of disrespect this would show to actual priests. I can think of few things funnier than Richard Dawkins taking to dressing like the Pope while lecturing and presenting science programmes). The pay is amazing. Roughly £100 per ceremony, five to six a day over the weekend. Say 1,200 quid a weekend, 4,800 in an average four-weekend month. The guys I know who do this work a two-day week and are minted. Consequently, it's a locked world, jobs by recommendation only. You don't even need to be able to speak Japanese, just learn a phonetic script. The only qualification seems to be white skin and an overwhelming desire to never teach English ever again. I wouldn't advise it though, since you are dealing with what's supposed to be someone's happiest day. It can be nerve-wracking.

Kazuki's wedding is illustrative of this. My colleague Mike and I were the only non-Japanese guests. As we filed into the fake chapel, the priest was already at the altar, running lines. He was nervous, possibly this was his first. Sweat was beading on his brow and his hands were shaking. He'd clearly been clinging to one tiny shard of iceberg to keep him sane – that at least his audience would be a group of Japanese people who didn't know that he wasn't a real priest and taught English Monday to Friday. Then he looked up, glanced down the aisle, saw Mike and I approaching, and very loudly and very publicly announced from the altar, 'Oh, FUCK!'

Another priest I saw in action was a revelation. He'd embraced the ridiculousness of his role and despite being a Kiwi, as I found out chatting to him after, played the part of a cartoon Southern US evangelical preacher, all outrageous accent and 'Dear LORD, we BESEEECH Thee'. He was a hero and, with all due consideration to friends and family, this is still the best wedding I've ever attended.

Ours was nothing like this. First was the City Office, where the clerk kept trying to speak to me in Portuguese (there's a large Brazilian community near where Minori grew up and apparently I look Brazilian – Brazil famously being the home of overweight pasty blond men). The marriage was overseen by Minori's uncle, who is high up in the bureaucracy. He wished us well and handed over the traditional envelope of cash, then stood back with his arms folded while the clerk sweated over our forms. His presence really seemed to speed things along. We'd allocated a couple of hours for red tape but being related to the boss had a Mary Poppins effect on that paperwork and we were out of there in fifteen minutes flat.

If Minori had been in charge, that would have been that. We'd have swapped rings in the car park and been back at work before you could say, 'I do'. Fortunately, Dad and Catherine had come over from Hong Kong, where they were temporarily based, and that meant Minori had to buck her ideas up a bit and at least feign interest in the symbolism of the day.

We returned home. Minori changed into a kimono, with her mother's help (since it was a weekday the rest of her family had to work), and I put on a *yukata* – a thin summer kimono. My dad pulled on his kilt and we set off for Inuyama Castle.

This was my masterstroke. Inuyama Castle is one of only four original standing castles (the others are Matsumoto, Hikone and Himeji – the last famous for starring in *You Only Live Twice*). Inuyama was where I first lived in Japan. The castle is the symbol of the town and where we went on one of our first dates. It's also a beautiful spot for photos, with a secluded viewpoint overlooking the Kiso River. I got some champagne, some strawberries and some cold roasted wild boar (naturally) and we rocked up at the castle like the weirdest cosplay convention ever. My dad got papped all the way through town, since clearly they'd never seen a man in a tartan skirt before, and a small crowd gathered around us at the castle (we hadn't told them we were coming or what we were planning) as we swapped rings, took photos and toasted the future. Some of the onlookers offered to take pictures of the whole group, particularly one helpful old man who framed us perfectly from the nose down.

In the evening, the rest of the clan joined us and we partied like it was 2009. Dad and Yoji got on like a Sambuca on fire, men in their late fifties being famously able to communicate across language barriers using only the twin powers of alcohol and toasts. I did a speech, a short paragraph in Japanese, and that was that. The day ended with tight handshakes, deep meaningful stares and patiently waiting taxi drivers.

I can't move on from the subject of weddings in Japan without a tip of the hat to Francis's brother, who flew over from England to deliver the best man's speech with the aid of a translator.

Twelve tables. Ten of Japanese guests, one of foreigners and their Japanese partners, one of Francis's family. His brother Phil delivered his speech, very much in the tradition of a British best man speech. This is something Japan failed to carry across, so ten tables had no idea what they were getting. Would it be like a boss's speech, or perhaps like a friend's *kampai* speech: a quick congratulations and cheers? Nope, it was jokes. Ribald jokes. Jokes insulting the groom. They were good jokes, and the two English-speaking tables responded enthusiastically. The translator did a good job but humour is hard to translate. (An anecdote: when President Jimmy Carter delivered a speech in Japan he opened with a joke but quickly realised it probably wouldn't translate well. However, he was already midway through and felt he had to finish. To his great surprise, upon delivering the punchline the room erupted in laughter. Afterwards he said to his translator, 'You did a wonderful job with the joke. How did you manage it?' The translator replied, 'Easy. I said, "President Carter has just made a joke. You must laugh now."').

Phil reached his closer. 'And I have to say that Ayaka is an amazing woman, way better than Francis deserves, and way better than any of the other Asian mail-order brides he tried before.'

The English-speaking tables laughed loudly.

The translator began to translate. Word for word.

Everyone at our table, the bilingual table, started waving their arms at the translator and mouthing, 'No! No!'

Too late.

Silence. A thoroughly displeased father of the bride. Awkwardness for the rest of the evening.

Guerrilla speeches. Get in, get out, and if you're going to drop a bomb don't hang around to witness the damage.

In the October of our first year in the countryside, there were no specific festivities, but the two fathers quickly resumed their saké-and-cheers-ing relationship, this time around my fire pit. We organised the biggest barbecue to date, possibly the biggest the village has ever seen. All of Minori's family, the Asais, the estate agent who helped us find the place, some friends. As is the rural way, others simply dropped by with cans or meat in tow. We started at lunchtime and went late into the night, the fire blazing – as were the guests. The number of children climbing the trees seemed to grow to Peter Pan proportions. Yoji took a dislike to a tree that was hanging a bit too much over the road and, mid-barbecue, after a few sakés, attacked it with an axe. I got the guitar out and played so my dad could sing, Zeppelin mostly. He has a good voice and great taste in music, having seen the likes of Zeppelin and The Who back in the day. Around 4 p.m. I looked out over the garden. The trees were still full of children. Dad and Yoji were gesticulating and communicating somehow. Catherine, Minori, Chiharu, Atsuko and Miyoko were deep in a discussion about education styles (Catherine teaches at primary school, Chiharu taught kindergarten, and Atsuko is the head teacher of a kindergarten). The rest of the men were stretched out on blankets or laid back in chairs fast asleep – a great sign of respect, which says 'I am happy, content, full, relaxed and comfortable in my surroundings, so much so that I am going to take a nap here'.

I felt great joy at that moment, probably more than at any other time since moving. Our families were enjoying each other's company, the garden was being used for its main purpose – as a place where happiness can bloom – and there was no place in time or space I would rather have been than there. Minori and I had made a home, we had found our place, carved out our niche, settled in. We'd been accepted by our neighbours (what better sign of acceptance is there than a child you've never seen before hanging upside down from one of your trees, their parents clearly not at all worried where they are or what they are doing, knowing they'll be fine) and I'd been accepted by Minori's family. More, I'd been able to show all this to my father. You don't need a speech at a wedding thanking your parents for raising you, caring for you. You just need a moment like that: here I am, this is what I've done with the life you gave me. I took on board everything you said, even if it didn't seem so at the time, and this is the result. This barbecue, these people, this life.

冬

Winter

Winter Wooksie

'How's winter in your country? Cold?'

I'm a hater of stereotypes and will usually take a contrary position to one on general principle. 'How's winter in your country? Cold?' Actually, it's . . . No, I can't back that up.

Pretty much, yep. It is cold, and dark, and wet. But if you strip everything down to bare stats, the winters in Scotland and Gifu are pretty similar. Temperatures hovering just above zero for the most part, with occasional dives below. Snow in the hills, the odd day of it in the towns; places for skiing but little disruption of work or school. The difference is that winter in Gifu is sunny, clear skies, very little rain. Not so much Scotland. It's a simple fact of latitude. Where I was born: 57-ish degrees north. Where I am now: 35-ish degrees north. That's 22-ish whole degrees of difference. For reference that's the difference between Aberdeen and Crete, Cyprus or Iran. The difference between Alaska and Texas. That's a big ol' chunk of the Earth. The Gulf Stream mediates a bit, but dark nights and a coastline open to the Atlantic mean winter is not the ideal time to be in Scotland. Going to and from school in darkness was one of the more depressing aspects of my childhood.

So yeah, on paper winter in southern Gifu and northern Scotland are similar. But lots of things on paper are misleading.

After the excesses of summer here, you'd think I'd welcome winter, and for the first couple of years I did. But you can become used to everything, and as I mentioned before the sudden drop in temperature that people insist on calling 'autumn' gives winter a stronger bite than the raw data suggests.

Japanese houses are not built for warmth and ours is no exception. It's a bugbear all us immigrants have – or certainly the ones from outwith the Arctic Circle (my colleague from Alaska maintains 'this is nothing') – that building techniques seem positively primitive. Even the most basic homes in Aberdeen have thick granite walls, central heating throughout and multi-glazing. Not so in Japan. Modern houses have good glazing, and some even come with underfloor heating – though you still need to install air conditioners everywhere because underfloor cooling isn't a thing, costing you double – but the walls are wood and plaster. An old house in Japan means anything over ten years. Ours is twenty. It's not uncommon for it to be far warmer outside than in. We retreat to a couple of rooms, our electricity bill quadruples, and the whole place stinks of kerosene from the stoves.

I hate these things. I cannot sleep properly with cans of kerosene in the garage and a kerosene-filled bomb in the living room. Minori loves the heat they give off. I'm utterly terrified of a house fire. Our first winter here, a house in the next village went up, exactly for this reason (well, the hoarding nature of the owner made a fire much more likely by all accounts). Watching those flames gives my vague sense of unease a name and a face. Ironically, it gives me the shivers.

The reason for the lack of insulation isn't ignorance or stubbornness, as some assume after three days in the country. Rather, it's for the perfectly valid reason that there are a lot of earthquakes. Two or three earthquakes and around a thousand tremors *every day*. That is what geologists call 'a fucktonne'. Why on earth would you build out of something that could crack tomorrow, cost a fortune to repair, and if it fell on you would hurt quite a bit? No, you build out of wood and buy thicker socks. Though not the ones with individual toes because fuck those people. Seriously.

I do love the way winter looks in my garden, though. The air is crisper and clearer, meaning Mount Ontake is always sharp on the horizon, the snow on its jagged peak Himalayan in its beauty. I feel justified in including this as 'part of my garden', not because I am expressing ownership of Ontake, but because of the notion of 'borrowed scenery' (*shakkei*) in Japanese garden design. Simply put, you take into account the surrounding scenery when designing your garden. Forests, hills, mountains, lakes, rivers, castles, whatever may be beyond your boundaries can be referenced in the shaping of the garden. For more on this, read Tan Twan Eng's fabulous *The Garden of Evening Mists* which goes into the aesthetic of it far better than I ever could.

So through the gap in the trees on the east side of my garden Ontake stands like some benevolent god overlooking the world (though as mentioned elsewhere, Ontake isn't all that benevolent). Inside the frontiers of my world, winter is splendid. The previous owner's grandfather, who designed the garden, is represented today by a small shrine that still stands and which, for some unknown reason, infuriates the crows who claim fiefdom over the garden. Almost every day I have to pick up the little ornaments that adorn the shrine from where the crows have cast them. I sometimes wonder if the birds are trying to warn us of something, but then I think they just like sitting on the shrine and the ornaments get in the way and I've just watched too much *Game of Thrones*. Trees were strategically planted to block and channel wind, a fact I appreciated more in 2018 when a series of massive typhoons hurtled through Gifu. He also took great care in choosing seasonal plants and trees, meaning that the garden never has a fallow period, that there is perpetual blooming (which would be my tagline to the annual Bloomsday festival in Dublin).

Winter sees the blossoming of *sazanka* (camellia in English), red rosette-like flowers that stand out against the sombre winter colours like stars in the night sky. The autumn leaves lie where they fell, making a carpet of burgundy and gold, and on the days when it snows lightly, the frosting is perhaps one of the most heart-warming things in nature. During these months there is no greater pleasure than heading outside with a bottle of Chilean red, a nice bobble hat and thick boots, to get the fire roaring, and just sitting in that winter stillness breathing in the calmness of the season, the moment when nature inhales and collects itself before the exhalation of spring.

In My Tree

Winter for the amateur farmer and gardener in Japan means – like a tour cyclist cresting a hill just as the EPO kicks in – a change of pace. Coming from Scotland, one thing I'll never get my head around is growing vegetables in winter. It's cold, the ground is covered in frost, sometimes frozen solid, and there's much less sunlight, yet somehow the vegetables survive. All things being equal.

Carrots, onions, garlic and potatoes. There are a number of variables to take into account when you're starting out and, unsurprisingly, the internet is awash with conflicting advice. My neighbours were just as helpful as the worldwide web.

'You want to use this kind of weedkiller.'

'You don't want to use any weedkiller but you're going to have to weed it every day.'

'Don't worry about the weeds. There's a new type of farming which is much more holistic. The weeds and the vegetables develop a harmonious relationship.'

'Those runs are too close together.'

'Those runs are too far apart. You could fit another one in between.'

'Too cold.'

'Too shady.'

'You need to water those.'

'They look like they're drowning.'

'You're doing it wrong.'

'You're doing it wrong.'

'You're doing it wrong.'

*

I was doing it wrong, almost certainly, but I was fine with that. I have, entropy willing, forty-ish years to get it right. The best way to learn is trial and error.

My first mistake was the potatoes. I watched a video of a hale and hearty Irishman planting and harvesting his tatties, and did what he said, adjusting for a different climate. The idea of winter growing is that you put things in early enough so that they sprout and get settled in, get comfy, and then over the cold winter months they store energy ready for a spring burst. For things like carrots, this gives them a ripe, sweet flavour. My carrots come up green and bushy, exactly like a Bugs Bunny cartoon. I end up with way too many onion shoots in my seed trays, green and red ones, and find myself filling every available slot with them. The garlic takes hold and immediately attracts every weed in the area. Garlic is a nitrogen fixer, most other plants are nitrogen users. Like junkies around a dealer, the weeds gather. The tatties burst into a thick green canopy worryingly quickly. I watch the Irishman again. Yep, too quickly. It must be some weird side effect of the climate, a mistake in my calculations. Sure enough, a few weeks later, when the first frost hits and the patch on the north side of the house freezes into concrete, the leaves wilt and die.

Arse.

I avoid the neighbours, avoid 'I told you so'. Trial and error. I tried. I erred.

Around me, the proper farmers have harvested the rice, the stalks are burned and the fields are bereft of all but stubble. The cycle of growth and bloom has entered its fallow period, and the weeds have given their upwardly mobile nonsense a bloody rest. There is some respite from the regular chores but no rest for the committed. Our attention turns to those jobs long put aside.

Two things have been hanging around my to do list like bored teenagers in an underpass, filling me with more dread than one of my favourite celebrities suddenly trending on Twitter. The trees need pruning and the corner needs napalming.

My land is roughly rectangular, running longways from road to road, and bounded by Asai on one side and by Sasaki and Hasegawa on the other. However, for some bizarre reason known only to history and bureaucracy, Asai's land is about ten metres shorter than mine. Beyond his newly planted orange trees, there are about four metres of no man's land owned – on paper at least – by Gifu Prefecture. As far as I can tell, no one from the Prefecture Office or the City Office has ever been to see or, more importantly, tend this land, and so Asai and I take turns to keep the bamboo, parasitic vines and other assorted chlorophyll-toting pests at bay. The remaining four metres are mine, a jagged hangnail off an otherwise geometrically pleasing shape.

Due to the remains of several tree stumps (from before my time) and the proximity of a sharp drop down to a relatively busy road, I'm at a loss over what to do with this spit of land. Asai's grandkids use it as a short-cut to school, and in order to avoid entanglement both literal and legal, I need to go at it machete first. The problem here is that Yamada lives on the other side of the road and he's a talker. Retired, with his sole daughter and grandkids living in China after her husband was transferred, and a wife who, in his words, 'doesn't like me very much, at least not since I retired', he's always on the lookout for a good natter. He's a nice guy and I've had many interesting chats with him – he's one of the few old men around here who understands how to modulate his language so I can follow him. The others can be as impenetrable as a White House statement of clarification. However, like an over-elaborate series of similes, once he starts he's very difficult to stop. So, like Nigel de Jong in the 2010 World Cup, I'll get about ten minutes' quality hacking done before being halted. The key is to do it on a rainy day, when the weather will keep him at bay, but winter here tends to be dry.

In the meantime, the trees need a haircut. Next to Asai's house are two enormous cherry trees. The blossom is stunning – the previous owners showed us pictures as the season was over by the time we moved in – and I'm loth to do anything to damage the trees. Cherry trees are notoriously difficult creatures, and lopping off limbs can leave them exposed to all manner of fungi and insects. I was hoping to put this off for a few years but my hand has been forced. At the end of September, a typhoon blundered through Gifu and revealed a hitherto unexpected bendiness to the trees. Both *sakura* cherry trees headbanged against Asai's roof, fortunately leaving no damage but scaring the shit out of everyone inside and leading to Asai's request to give them a trim. Which I'd be very happy to do if the tops weren't so far from the ground. The main problem is one of height. The trees are taller than Asai's three-storey house, and if we snip lower down, they'll just fall through into someone's bedroom.

Someone will have to go up there, and as sure as Piers Morgan needs a dose of Ebola, it wasn't going to be me.

Me and heights. We don't see eye to eye.

I used to be fine. As a kid I'd climb trees, jump off walls, haul myself up the drainpipe onto the school roof to retrieve footballs with nary a thought for what Newton could do to me. But with age has come a greater respect for the ground in all its hard, rocky forms. I've learned to deal with it, even to push myself in the hope that exposure will cure me (a theory that led to me climbing the Eiffel Tower via the stairs. The metal ones with huge gaps in them so you can see what isn't beneath you. I wouldn't go so far as to say it worked, but I didn't die, so there.)

The peak, as it were, of my fear came about six weeks into my relationship with Minori. We went on our first date on 15 November 2006 and her birthday is in December. Bad timing, I know. A new relationship, still getting to know each other, and suddenly two present-giving occasions in quick succession. I am not a good present-giver. I have no imagination in this direction. If you don't want alcohol or a gift card, I'm no use to you. I suggested we go away, our first overnighter as a couple.

'Sure. Where should we go?'

'I don't know. Where's good in winter?'

'We could go skiing?'

'Can you ski?'

'I used to when I was a kid. You?'

'Same. Maybe we should put that to one side. How about a nice warm hotel in a nice warm city? Tokyo? Yokohama? Kyoto? Kobe?'

'Could do.'

'What do Japanese couples usually do in this situation? Where do they go?'

'Disneyland. Or Universal Studios.'

'Seriously?'

'Yep.'

'Want to do that?'

'You want to go to Disneyland?'

'No, I'm asking if you want to go. It's your birthday.'

'It's busy just before Christmas. You know what you're like with queues.'

'Midweek? Remember my days off are Tuesday and Wednesday.'

'That might be okay. All right, let's go to Disneyland.'

See where trying to be a nice guy gets you? A day in Disneyland and a day in DisneySea. Fucksake.

It wasn't that bad. In the early days of a relationship, doing something you don't want to do but your partner does has a way of reaping rewards, and after riding the Tower of Terror I needed rewarding. For those who don't know, the Tower of Terror is a freefall ride. Framed by the usual haunted house nonsense, you enter an elevator, strap yourself in and are dropped so that you get an adrenaline rush and revisit what you had for breakfast. Thanks to a seventy-minute wait I had psyched myself up for the drop. I'd heard it was in the dark and figured that would be fine. The thing about a fear of heights is that you tend to have to see how far away the ground is before you can be scared of it. Darkness? Nae bother.

So we get in. It goes up. And up. And up. Then the doors open. We are on top of the tower, looking out over the Tokyo skyline and Tokyo Bay.

We sit there admiring the view just long enough for the height to register and then, like a Beastie Boys beat, they let

us

drop.

*

Next to the Tower of Terror is a decommissioned cruise liner converted into a restaurant and bar. I wobble over, Minori in my wake.

'Whisky.'

'Yes, sir, we have . . .'

'Any whisky.'

'Here you are, sir.'

'. . . ahhh. And another.'

So I'm not going up in the trees. Yoji, Minori and I ponder the situation.

'Let's just hire a professional with a cherry-picker.'

'They're expensive.'

'So is treatment for ninety-seven broken bones and a new roof for Asai.'

'I'll do it.'

'No, Dad. It's too high.'

'No, look . . .' He's got this *A-Team* gleam in his eye. 'I can get up onto there via the ladder. Then using my harness, I can climb up to there. If I fashion a pole from bamboo and strap my saw to the end of it then I can reach those branches and if Iain's over there pulling on a rope, the branches will swing out away from the house. Easy.'

Somewhere the ghost of Isaac Newton is rubbing his hands in expectation.

A couple of weeks later, I'm standing beside a cypress sapling, rope wrapped around my fists, arms taut, waiting. Yoji is up in the branches and even at this distance I can see he realises he's literally and figuratively out on a limb. He unclips his harness to shimmy onto a new branch and I hold my breath until I hear the carabiner click back in. Asai takes hold of the rope in front of me, rendering my grip redundant but I happily let him – if this branch goes the wrong way, it'll smash through his kitchen window. If he wants skin in the game, he can have it. Riku, Asai's ten-year-old grandson, is getting in the way, swishing fallen branches like swords, climbing other trees and generally ignoring pleas to back up and watch his head.

'This isn't going to work,' Yoji calls down. As he's sawn halfway through the branch, it's a bit late to give up.

'Why?'

'When it drops, the main branch will go that way, but it'll swivel as it does, and those branches will go straight into the house.'

He's right. 'How about if I stand over that side?'

'It'll help a bit but not enough.'

'Another rope?'

'I can't get out there to tie it – I've cut too far for it to take my weight.' He shifts slightly and a very audible creak comes from the limb.

'I've got an idea.' Asai lets go of the rope and disappears into his own garden, behind his shed. Presumably Yoji can see what he's up to but all I can hear are clanks and clangs. Suddenly the twin prongs of a ladder appear over the shed roof, followed by the sweating bald head of Asai.

'Careful,' Yoji calls to him. The metal roof is pretty solid and the shed clearly well-constructed, but Asai is a well-built man in his seventies and really shouldn't be up there.

'Pass me the bamboo.' The pole with the saw tied to it is about four metres long and looks like something Robinson Crusoe would use to catch Moby Dick. Trying not to spear Asai, Yoji passes it to him. Asai unties the saw and hooks one end of the rope through the two chopstick-like prongs that held the saw and passes the other end back to Yoji. He takes it and deftly drops it over the end of the branch closest to the house. With the kind of flick that wouldn't look out of place in a martial arts movie, he reconnects with the end of the rope, hooks it around another branch so it is secure and lowers it to Asai. We now have two ropes in place, mine pulling the main branch down and away, Asai's pulling the top branches out, effectively spinning the whole thing away from the house.

'Ready?'

'Ready.'

'Ready.'

A few quick strokes of the saw, a timbersome creak and it falls. I yank my rope and run backwards while Asai reels his in, somehow managing to keep his balance on the shed roof. The branches whip round, missing the house, but my rope comes free, leaving the main, heavy branch to obey Newton. It slams into the ground and rolls back, sending the trailing branches directly into Asai's path. Like Kilgore in *Apocalypse Now*, he stands his ground as twigs and leaves rain around him and the roof reverberates. I freeze, but he's unscathed and already has his own saw out, clearing his shed. Yoji rests his head against the bark and gives me a look of thank fuck.

Riku and his younger sister Sora play in a nest of felled branches while Yoji, Asai, Kensuke and I sip well-earned beers.

'That should be enough for a while,' I say.

'If we cut back any more, it'll really damage the tree,' says Yoji. 'Any more and we might as well just cut the whole thing down.'

'No, don't do that,' says Kensuke. 'They're beautiful in spring.'

'You're going to have to get used to heights then, Iain.'

'Why's that?'

'They'll eventually grow back, and by the time they do, I won't be able to go up there again.'

'Do you know anyone selling a second-hand cherry-picker?'

'I'll ask around.'

'Is that you done?' says Kensuke.

'No,' I say. 'That one's going to be trouble by next year.'

'Is it cherry blossom?' says Yoji.

'No,' says Asai. 'It's a *ginkgo*.'

'Iain, do you want it pruned or just taken out?'

'It's too close. Might as well just take it all out. Chainsaw it.'

'Good.'

'Why?'

'I can keep my feet on the ground.'

Gold Sounds

Homonyms. The curse of the language learner. You learn one word and suddenly it turns out it means something else. Seal and seal. Sign and sign. Chips and chips and chips and chips. The first homonym you learn in Japanese is *hashi*. It can mean bridge or chopstick. No connection, just infinite use of a finite set of syllables. This is where *kanji* – the Chinese logograms – come in handy. Written down, there is no confusion. 橋 (bridge) 箸 (chopsticks). Easy peasy. Um.

Tako. Octopus. I can't eat octopus, which is a shame because it's everywhere in Japan – the food, not the actual animal. The country isn't overrun with leggy molluscs, just the restaurants. I can't eat it because when I was at university in Aberdeen I made the mistake of going to the supermarket with a hangover. As I passed the seafood counter a friend (I can't remember who, I suspect Robert) spotted something and picked it up, showed it to me. It wasn't Irn-Bru or black pudding so initially I took no notice. Then I took notice. It was a tiny octopus, about the size of a mobile phone, whole and intact, shrink-wrapped, its rubbery face and big eye stretched by the magic mirror of clingfilm. I only just made the toilet before vomiting. No octopus. Ever.

But I learned the word. Tako. *Takoyaki* – octopus ball. On sale at festivals. A party food, a favourite of Minori and her friends. *Tako* sashimi. *Tako* sushi. *Tako* salads. *Takotsubo*. No, not that one. I just googled that. It means cardiomyopathy. My word for the day. Useful.

Tako. As used in the following sentence.
見って! たこが飛んでいる!

This sentence was uttered by my nephew Haru when he was about three or four years old. Standing in the garden of Minori's parents' house. He pointed at the sky, delighted. 'Look! An octopus is flying!'

What? I mean. What?

I look. No octopus. Obviously. Is this kid an idiot? I look at everyone else. No one seems confused. A few others are looking, smiling. Are they humouring him? I ask Minori.

'What did he say?'

'たこが飛んでいる'

Nope. No help there. I'm clearly missing something. In Japan do octopuses fly? Is he talking about cloud shapes? I look again but there are no clouds. It's a beautiful, clear day. Nothing in the sky apart from a kite.

Ah. *Tako* = kite.

The Flying Octopus would be a good name for a bar.

Crazy Train

Trains are big in Japan. The home of the Shinkansen, the trains run on time and are clean – unimaginably utopian for a wide-eyed boy from Britain. There is an argument that the worst thing that ever happened to the rail network in Britain was to have avoided invasion and extreme bombardment during the Second World War. Our Victorian network survived the war and has never been comprehensively rebuilt while the countries that now have excellent networks – Japan, Germany, France, the Netherlands – all had their networks decimated and had to start again. Britain needs a good slate cleaning.

Trainspotting is a popular pastime in Japan, and on the route from the city out towards where we live there are a few famous stations where train photographers gather to get scenic snaps of rolling stock with temples, autumn leaves or cherry blossom in the background. There are two main images of rail travel in Japan: the sleek, futuristic, duck-faced bullet trains that zip across the country at the kind of speeds that would make Thomas the Tank Engine shit himself (Nagoya to Tokyo, one hour forty-five minutes; Glasgow to Liverpool, same distance, about 260km, and an average of four hours assuming no delays, random stops or single-cell organisms on the line) and jam-packed subways, with people wedged in like disclaimers at the end of a pay-day lender's advert. Japanese stations have been known to employ shovers during rush hour, men whose sole job is to push as many people as possible into the carriages, like Minori packing a suitcase for an overnight trip.

I've experienced the shoving, and while it's uncomfortable, there's something levelling about it – all commuters are suffering the same tight misery, face shoved into armpits with bags in your kidneys – although being a good foot taller than the average commuter I suffer less than those around me, especially in summer. The shoving does occasionally lead to moments of embarrassment. I remember once riding the Yamanote line in Tokyo – the circle line that encapsulates the city and runs through some of the busiest stations in the world, including Shinjuku, which, with an average of 3.5 million people passing through every day, is officially the busiest in the world and a godawful place to try to navigate – and by sheer chance managed to get a seat. A few people got on at Meguro, a few more at Ebisu, then we hit Shibuya and the hordes flooded in and in and in. It never seemed to end. You could feel the air being pushed out of the carriage. If we'd been in a cartoon the train would have swollen up like a link of sausages. Eventually, the doors closed with all the strain of my belt buckle after Christmas dinner and we set off. Harajuku was only a few minutes away and surely some would get off there, but no. Apparently – I couldn't see anything from my seat – more got on, clambering over the top presumably. At Yoyogi the same thing, only this time something had to give. Unfortunately, that something was the poor young woman standing in front of me. The crowd shifted. She moved with it, lost her footing and fell. Fell, forward and down, twisting as she did so, landing with a bump to end up sitting in my lap. The crowd spilled into the micro space she had vacated, and she was stuck. I acted immediately, shifting my bag and raising my hands above my head so there was no danger of being accused of taking advantage of the situation.

She tried to get up, couldn't. She was clearly mortified and there was little I could offer in comfort. There is a young woman sitting in my lap. What do you say?

'I'm sorry,' she said.

'I'm sorry,' I replied.

Which is the only thing you can say that doesn't in some way sound creepy.

We sat through probably some of the most uncomfortable minutes in either of our lives while those around us smiled in polite Schadenfreude. Eventually, decades later, we arrived at Shinjuku and the carriage emptied for a moment, allowing her to escape and me to lower my hands from the safety position.

Japanese trains have female-only carriages now, and I have some sympathy for this. Even without perverts (arse-grabbing, up-skirt photographing weirdos), shovers and gravity can lead to non-consensual proximity.

So these are the two main images of Japanese trains people have, but there is a third: the country line. Single-carriage one-man trains or two-carriage locals for rush hour. They frequently run empty, and every passenger seems to know each other. When I first came to Japan I had to take one of these to and from work, shifts which invariably ran from 12 to 8 p.m. On the way in, the trains were reasonably busy, but often in the evening my Kiwi flatmate Darius and I were the only passengers. Despite this, the ever professional staff still performed their duties to the highest and most rigorous levels, pointing at every sign and announcing every station and safety warning, even though they probably thought we couldn't comprehend a word of it. *Au contraire*, train men, my first Japanese language classes were those commutes, when I tuned my ears to the echoey PA announcements and mastered intransitives (the doors are closing), imperatives (stand behind the yellow line) and polite forms (*densha ga mairimasu* – the train is coming).

One evening, Darius and I were the only two passengers. We were sitting at the very back of the last carriage, in front of the guard's window. Usually there is a driver at the front and a guard at the back. It's the guard who does all the announcements, opens and closes the doors, and walks through the train checking everything's train-shape and Stevenson fashion. This time the guard was a young trainee, out on stabilisers under the guidance of his very own Mr Miyagi. This wasn't the usual performance – this was a *performance*, a young trainee no doubt put upon by the master-student relationship that still permeates society, out on a limb, forever seconds away from failure, his boss looking for the slightest slip, the slightest sign of lack of focus, a detail forgotten, a stage skipped. The last thing this train-ee needed was two foreigners taking the piss.

The stops on this line are close together, and usually the announcements are curtailed to the briefest information. *The next stop is . . . This is . . . The doors are closing.* But he couldn't do that. He had to do the full script. *Ladies and gentlemen, welcome to . . .* Invariably, he was still halfway through welcoming the invisible passengers from one station when we pulled in at the next. First we giggled. Then we laughed. Then we started giving thumbs up, encouragement, rounds of applause. Over his shoulder we saw his teacher laughing, which just egged us on more. When we finally pulled into Inuyama he got a standing ovation and a pat on the back from his boss.

We can be real dicks sometimes.

On more than one occasion Darius and I would skip home entirely, going straight from work to Nagoya where we'd meet up with Francis, Thom and the others for an evening of bridge and tiffin. Something a lot of people don't know is that an empty train is in many ways a lot like a changing room. In that you can change in it. Taking advantage of the partition between carriages blocking us from the guard, and the driver's attention being on the tracks, we'd get out of our suits and into our best pulling gear between stations. One time, the guard took an impromptu stroll through the train and came upon the sight of me with besuited top half, jeans in hand, trousers on the seat next to me, boxer shorts on display.

'Good evening,' I said. 'Hot today, isn't it?'

He returned to his cabin and never ventured forth again.

Our village in Gifu is linked to the world by a JR line. The station is so tiny it doesn't even have a ticket machine or gate. What it does have is endless entertainment. Nearby is a care home for people with intellectual disabilities, and the residents often ride the train back and forth in pairs and threes, having a fine day out without all the messy business of actually having to go anywhere. They are all very sweet people who love a good chat, and they often single me out for special attention, intrigued by this foreigner in their midst but unencumbered by concerns over social niceties that stop others from asking outright, 'Who are you and why are you here?'

One of my favourites is Shinzo, a man in his sixties who I suspect has extreme Asperger's. I've chatted to him a couple of times, the usual stuff about weather and where I'm from, and yes, some people there are taller than me, yes, really, and he is harmless. Unfortunately, some well-meaning person at some point in his history has attempted to explain social rules to him. He has latched on to these as absolute commandments that must be obeyed at all times. One of them, possibly given to him by a mischievous or just old-fashioned gentleman, is 'always welcome and introduce yourself to young women'.

The train arrives. Stops. Shinzo presses the door open button repeatedly until it does what he wants. He steps on and looks up and down the length of the carriage. He notes the number and location of all the young, pretty girls and gets to work.

'Good morning. My name is Yamaguchi Shinzo. It is a pleasure to meet you.'

He doesn't even wait for a response, just moves on to the next person. Often the women are in groups or pairs, and he repeats the same speech to each in turn. Once he is satisfied he has done his duty, he takes a seat next to whoever he is travelling with that day and never again so much as glances at the women again. The first time you see it, it looks creepy as all hell, but there seems to be absolutely nothing sexual in it. Someone has given him an instruction about social interaction and he's damned if he's going to break the rules. In some ways, it's sweet. In others, it's hilarious.

'Who was that!'

A group of high school girls are on their way into the city on a Saturday morning.

'Oh, that's Shinzo. He's harmless.'

'Harmless? He's creepy.'

'He's fine. He just introduces himself to all the cute girls.'

'Eh? He didn't introduce himself to me!'

Refuse/Resist

For all its faults, I will say this about social media: it has made the reality of living on the other side of the world far easier. I write this in Dublin Airport, returning home to Japan after a two-week stint overseeing exchange students at Dublin City University. The place has changed a lot since I was last there, in 2007. One of the big changes I noticed is how they have really got their act together about remembering and commemorating the famine and the reality of Irish emigration. The EPIC Irish Emigration Museum, the *Jeanie Johnston* 'coffin' ship and the famine memorial along the Liffey do a wonderful job of bringing together the facts, the horror and the silver linings of forced emigration. I found myself wondering why Scotland doesn't have something similar. Somewhere in the Highlands perhaps, or maybe by Greenock or Gourock, somewhere the Clearance ships left from. Or in Glasgow, Edinburgh maybe, somewhere more people could go. A museum, a memorial, somewhere the whole damn story could be told, unfragmented, for good and bad.

Because every immigrant story is also an emigrant story. This is what the Right want us to forget. They want us to believe it's all about them coming here, not about them leaving there. Japan is particularly guilty of this, with a stunning twenty refugees out of 16,929 applications being granted asylum in 2017.

One line in the EPIC Museum kept battering round my head for days afterwards, and I still hear it now as I sit in a coffee shop at departures being served by people who have come to Ireland for a better life.

We go because we have to.

We go because we must.

We go because we have no choice.

I'm lucky. I was born white, male, rich (comparatively by world standards, not really by the divided standards of late capitalist UK) and free. Privilege upon privilege upon privilege. I had a choice: I could have had a good life in Scotland, in Europe, America or Australia. I chose a good life in Japan. My reasons for living on the other side of the world are petty and irrelevant in comparison with those who went because they had to.

That difference, that crucial, fundamental difference will always separate me from them. I cannot sit with a Syrian refugee, or a Cambodian labourer sending every penny back to their family, or an LGBTQ+ Russian unable to go home, and say, 'Yes, I know how you feel.' I don't. Of course I don't. I can imagine, though. I'm a novelist; it's literally in the job description to imagine the lives of others, but imagining and *knowing* are not the same. I cannot offer understanding. But I can be an ally. I can offer solidarity.

Immigrants are immigrants are immigrants. There is no such thing as a good immigrant or a bad immigrant. There are good people and bad people. Arseholes over there and arseholes over here. Arseholes like to travel. I'm in an airport right now, and there are arseholes everywhere. There was a guy in front of me at the security queue ranting about a twenty-minute delay when he'd be crossing the Atlantic in a matter of hours. Another, a businessman, refused to take off his watch and belt, to put his loose change in the box at the metal detector because clearly he was so much more special than the rest of us. God bless the young Irish woman who just kept sending him back again and again until this pathetic man had to admit that he had no authority and that his anger was irrelevant. But the fact that someone is an arsehole has nothing to do with their distance from the place of their birth or the source of their nationality. If you want to separate immigrants into two camps, there's one way: those who chose and those who didn't. Those who go because they must and those who go because they want to.

The world right now demonises those who had no choice, but is fine with those like me, the rich, white, free ones. We even have different names. They are immigrants: we are expats.

The British media has managed to muddy the waters so much that all immigrants are illegal, unwelcome, dangerous. The same outlets worry about the poor British expats in Spain who might be inconvenienced by the simple fact of Brexit.

Immigrants are them: expats are us.

Let's be clear: this is racism. The term 'expat' is encoded racism. British expats in Dubai. Middle Eastern immigrants in Britain. The expat community in Spain. Areas overrun by immigrants in Birmingham. Expats are rich, free, white. Immigrants are poor, have limited choices and are rarely white.

A conversation a white German friend of mine had with a dick in the run-up to Brexit.

Dick: There are too many immigrants here.

Friend: You mean like me.

Dick: No, you're not an immigrant.

Friend: I'm German. I moved here ten years ago.

Dick: No, you're an expat. I'm talking about immigrants. You know . . .

At this point he waved a hand over his face signifying 'skin colour'. You can spot immigrants, you see. They stand out, and that's just not on. They don't even have the courtesy to try and fit in, physically. Dick.

This section is the only time you will see the word 'expat' in this book. I reject the label my privilege buys me in order to ally myself with those who go because they must. I too am an immigrant. When you demonise immigrants, include me in their number. Demonise me. If you truly think people should remain all their lives in the country of their birth, then be consistent. The French billionaire based in the Cayman Islands, the British oil worker in Dubai, the Scottish teacher in Japan, the

Bangladeshi waiter in your local curry house and the Syrian child in Yarl's Wood Immigration Removal Centre. All immigrants.

If you absolutely must be nice to some and nasty to others, why not be nasty to those of us riding the wave of privilege and save your empathy for those who go because they must?

I talk to my friends daily on Facebook and WhatsApp. I chat with my mum on Skype as often as the time difference allows. I read the news as it happens and watch events unfold. I can be more involved in British political life than many of those who live there, given so many dribble nonsense about 'them all being the same' and how none of us can have any effect on the process. Compared with a hundred years ago, when ships took weeks and months to arrive, letters contained news long out of date, and moving abroad could mean never seeing your friends and family ever again, we're living in a utopia. It does have its drawbacks though. Ignorance, or at least delayed awareness, can indeed be bliss.

The first summer I was in Japan, Al-Qaeda bombed London. I came back from work oblivious, went online. The words 'bomb' and 'London' caught my eye, but I didn't think too much about it. I typed out a bland and pointless blog, posted it, checked my emails: one from GNER advertising discount travel, one from Channel 4 advertising some film, and one phishing for my bank details – three emails trying to get money from me, one at least showing some initiative. Went to the BBC News site (I still did that then, before the Scottish Referendum and Brexit, when the BBC understood what 'non-biased' meant) and saw the headline, the pictures.

Disconnected amazement, resigned acceptance, well, it was gonna happen at some point. Then it clicks. London. London isn't an abstract concept, one of Chamberlain's faraway countries, home to people of whom we know nothing. Mike and Simon, they're there, in London, living, working. On to Messenger, Robert is the only one around, he's tried texting but hasn't heard back. Mike and Simon both work in the film industry, could be anywhere in the city. They're runners. Their job is to be everywhere. Safe. Unsafe.

As I sit there, desperate for information, unable to get any, it occurs to me that this is twice in less than a year. The worry on Boxing Day until the email from Fiona in Thailand, safe in the north, far from the tsunami.

Connection. Disconnection. It was news, something on TV, until I realised I might have skin in the game. It washed over me until I thought of Mike and Simon. Then it became real. Did it take fear for the safety of people I care about to make me care about the others? Yes, it did. I was too caught up in the implications – ID cards, racism, religious hatred, UK response – to see the people involved.

Is this how everyone reacts? That the implications of a terrorist attack are only filtered through the personal? It wasn't real until I thought of Mike – it was like reading about Stalingrad or Baghdad. Be it history or current events, it's people in a far-off country. The internet is supposed to bring us into the global village, but it's a village replete with a cast of idiots.

It's worth bearing in mind that when Chamberlain said, 'How horrible, fantastic, incredible it is that we should be digging trenches and trying on gas masks here because of a quarrel in a faraway country between people of whom we know nothing,' he was talking about Czechoslovakia, now an hour or so away by easyJet. Brits pride themselves on standing alone, on defending plucky little Poland during the Second World War. How many people in Britain in 1939 really cared about the people living in Poland? Three years earlier, only a brave few gave a crap about Spain and its fight against fascism. The mythology surrounding the Second World War may be the single most poisonous aspect of British identity. Little Britain, standing against the Third Reich. My grandfather was an RAF pilot. He once told me about getting into an argument down the pub one day, years ago, with an idiot who was going on about Eastern Europeans coming over here. Granddad pointed out that many of the pilots in the Battle of Britain were from Czechoslovakia and Poland (c. 230 out of 2,972, roughly 20 per cent, were 'non-British'). 'If it wasn't for the Czechs and the Poles,' my grandfather ended with a flourish, 'we'd all be speaking German.'

The London bombings, 2005. Once it hit me, the feeling stayed. If it took fear for their safety to make me *feel*, should news of their safety not take the feeling away? Maybe once it became real it couldn't become unreal. 'All your life you live so close to truth, it becomes a permanent blur in the corner of your eye, and when something nudges it into outline it is like being ambushed by a grotesque.' (*Rosencrantz and Guildenstern Are Dead*, Tom Stoppard)

Once you see it you can't 'unsee' it. The media filters everything for us, gives us the news in order of priority – one Briton injured, twelve others dead – so that it takes something extraordinary to make us see reality. I remember watching the amateur footage of a wedding in India, actually seeing the floor falling in and people plummeting to their deaths, hearing the screams and seeing the horror of the moment on people's faces – literally watching a terrified face disappear through the floor. It shocked us all deeply. 'Fifteen Die in Wedding Dancefloor Cave-in' would hardly have made a dent. Words are sometimes so inadequate.

I recall watching with fascination when the second plane hit the Twin Towers, the black dots falling from windows, and my thoughts were about Bush and who he would bomb. The idea that those black dots might be people came to me only vaguely. The Orson Welles speech in *The Third Man* about feeling pity if 'one of those dots stopped moving forever' seemed to sum it up perfectly.

Us and them. 'You always think this kind of thing happens to other people.' We are other people. They aren't dots. They aren't statistics. The world is falling apart, society fracturing, the planet burning. It's not us and them. It's us and us.

Comin' Under Fire

Many rural communities aren't covered by the main City Fire Brigade ('city' here being an administrative term and having nothing to do with population size, charters or cathedrals) and have stations run by part-time volunteers. The word 'volunteer', as in many formerly militaristic cultures, contains no connotation of free will here. Every man – always men – of age has to be trained and do a couple of years' service. As reservists, they can always be called on. Minori's brother had to suffer through this. My village has a part-time fire station but thus far no one has mentioned volunteering there to me. At one community association they had to appoint a fire safety officer. Another new resident, Kane-hara-san, raised his hand. 'I'm a full-time fire-fighter. It would make sense for me to do it.'

'Can you do it every year?'

'Sure.'

And that was that.

My friend John, who lives even deeper into the wilderness than me, is less fortunate but so far has resisted.

'I've been pushed to join the volunteer fire-fighters,' he told me, 'which is the main role for the majority of men around my age. Admittedly, it would be a good idea and some fun, but I'm not sure I can balance the time commitment right now. They understand if you have a proper reason to miss something, but if not, you need to be prepared to be a *gaijin* in the full meaning of the word, and never quite accepted. I'm finding that with the fire-fighters. They ask if I can join, and accept when I say no, but then they're not going to make a great effort to include me and my family in the local private events, when groups of friends have a barbecue, that sort of thing. It's a trade-off that I wasn't aware of before moving here, and I'm going to have to think about it now.'

Opt in, or opt out. Both choices have consequences.

It's not just the time commitments and language barriers (you're in a burning house, looking for trapped people, and it takes you a few seconds to remember if *migi* is left or right . . . Was that verb form an order, a suggestion or a negative conjugation? Should I stop or definitely *not* stop?), there are two other factors.

One is fear, fear based on a real awareness of the job. My father spent thirty years in the fire brigade. I've heard the stories. As kids, we went to the open days and saw demonstrations of how to put out a burning tower block, a car in flames, a crashed helicopter. Yes, helicopter, because this was Aberdeen, oil capital of Europe, base for the North Sea oil industry. My third novel, *The Waves Burn Bright*, is about the Piper Alpha disaster, the night when 167 people died 120 miles off the shore of Aberdeen. I researched. I read. I listened. I watched. I immersed myself in the stories of people who had jumped 180 metres into water that was on fire, people who crawled along flaming corridors with wet rags over their mouth, people who watched their friends and colleagues . . .

It gets inside your head, and it stays there. During our second year here, a house in the neighbouring village caught fire. We watched, helpless, horrified, as flames twice the height of the pine trees raged in the night sky. I double, triple-check if the gas is off, that the kerosene for the stove and the petrol for the lawnmower are secure, fastened tight, locked safely away in the garage. I love my fire pit, but I saturate the ground around it with water before lighting anything. The hose is on stand-by, leaves cleared in a wide circle.

That's the first reason: perfectly rational fear of what fire is, what it can do.

The second reason is less serious, less depressing, less terrifying, but no less important for all that: embarrassment.

See, in Japan, they like a 'way'. 道. *Dō*. A road, path, way, method. *Bushidō*, the way of the warrior. *Kendō*, the way of the sword. *Kyudō*, the way of the bow. *Judō*, the way of the Jew. There is a correct way of doing something, and many incorrect ways. Apprenticeships in Japan can last a decade. You don't learn roughly how to do something. You learn *exactly*. Before trains leave a station, the driver goes through a series of checks, literally saying each stage out loud and pointing in exaggerated gestures at the things he is checking. No short cuts. No improvisation, even if two half-naked *gaijin* are laughing at you. In Japan, if a train is more than twenty seconds late into a station, the driver is suspended and retrained. You do it right or you don't do it at all.

This is all very laudable, and the service industry (not to mention the privatised rail network) in the UK would do well to look to Japan's example, but there is a flip side. Sometimes it can be taken too far. Ways are invented just in order to have a way. Just in order to be seen to have a way. There is a correct way to conduct a ceremony. Fine. There is a correct way to be a samurai, a geisha, a monk. Yep, that makes sense. There is a correct way for a fire-fighter to enter and exit the fire engine.

Wait, what?

There is a way of walking, a way of moving, a way of comporting yourself while fighting a blaze.

And, honestly, it's fucking hilarious to see in action.

I first encountered the fireman's walk under a bridge at one o'clock in the morning.

When I moved to Japan in 2005, I was placed by my company in a town called Inuyama. About thirty minutes north of Nagoya on the Aichi/Gifu border, Inuyama is a sleepy commuter town with a long history and ambitions to be a big tourist destination. One of the four original surviving castles I mentioned earlier is in Inuyama (the rest were destroyed for various reasons and then rebuilt in attractive ferro-concrete), and in recent years they have done a brilliant job in promoting the town to tourists foreign and domestic, particularly its fabulous spring festival, more on which later.

I was the only teacher in my company placed in Inuyama. Most others lived in Nagoya. In some ways it was a lucky break – a modern two-bedroom flat to myself and the absence of English speakers meant I was forced to learn Japanese all the faster. The way it worked out though is that the friends I made in Nagoya were keen to expand their horizons and, once I discovered Kei's bar, people took to leaving the city rather than having me crash on their floor.

A favourite spot for a drink was under the bridge across the Kiso River. A couple of hundred metres along from the castle and about twenty minutes from my flat, it was perfect. Wide terraced levels had been built for the crowds who came every August for the fireworks festival so we had spacious, clean seating. The bridge – a road and rail bridge – was high enough that it wasn't cramped but low enough that it offered protection in the rain. It was perfect for all-night drinking and talking: no residents around, hidden from the road in case any cops wandered by. We spent many, many nights under that bridge, and quite a few days.

My first encounter with Japanese firemen was under this bridge with John, a Scouser who taught at the same school. (When I started I took over a kids' class from him. I showed the students, all about five years old, a flashcard with a picture of a book on it. 'What's this?' I asked. En masse they replied in a broad Scouse accent: 'It's a booch.' To be fair, when I left, the teacher who took over from me reported that the students responded to 'How are you?' by saying 'I'm grrrrreat' in an accent not unlike Mel Gibson's in *Braveheart*.) We'd have a few cans after work, some chat, a missed train, suddenly it was an all-nighter. I was twenty-five and all-nighters were still something I could not only manage but actively looked forward to. Today I take comfort in the knowledge that the last train is at 11 p.m., giving me a cast iron excuse to get home at a decent time. Back then, it wasn't beyond the realms of possibility that I 'mistook' the train times in order to partake in the great tradition of the all-nighter. It has been known. My eventual flat-mate in Inuyama, Darius, used the same trick at the end of dates.

So, one night, we went all Chili Peppers under the bridge there. As the clock approached one, and John and I still had enough in the carry-out, there came a rip of sounds and flashing lights. Cops! Quick! Hide the booze and pretend to be a monolingual simpleton! But no, it was a fire engine, red in tooth and claw. It edged down the slipway and pulled to a halt before us. John and I remained where we were, wondering what we'd done and what was going to be done to us. The men got out and fussed around the truck. We began to suspect their presence had nothing to do with ours. In fact, they seemed to not even know we were there. They lined up, military-style, to attention. Their leader barked a few orders and they set off at a march. At this point, John and I made our presence felt in the form of uproarious drunken laughter.

The Japanese fireman has an entirely unique form of locomotion. He starts in a standing position before leaning forward as if bowing. When movement begins, the arms piston alongside, the shoulder blades jutting, the fists pummelling downwards. The knees meanwhile are brought up sharply in turn to waist height, propelling the fireman forward. The overall effect is of a badly made but enthusiastic clockwork soldier taking off across the floor. It is hilarious, particularly when unleashed in the presence of unsuspecting drunks.

Startled and perhaps embarrassed, the men came to a sloppy halt. The leader gave us a dirty look and called the men into line. He drilled them for about twenty minutes, after which they piled back into the truck to a round of applause and disappeared into the night.

We later found out that one of the men, Hiro, was a friend of Kei's and drank in the bar. One day, a few months later, Kei's phone rang. It was Hiro.

'Run outside the shop!'

We obeyed. A fire truck, sirens and lights blazing sped by. Two firemen clung in position on the back. Well, one clung in position. The other was Hiro, fully kitted up, one arm and one leg in position, the others trailing behind the truck, star-shaped. The look of sheer joy on his chubby face as they roared by stays with me to this day. But on no account do I ever want to be in the position of having to march like a demented Donkey Kong beside a river in the early hours of the morning. No way.

*

Fifteen months later, Minori and I would have taken over as joint *hanchō*. She does the things that involve reading *kanji* and listening to extended complaints by local old men. I do the legwork: delivering notices round the houses, cleaning, organising the local festival. I come in from work at 7 p.m., tired, bedraggled, denied even the respite of beer due to a new fitness regime.

'Kanehara-san came round.'

'The fireman? Why?'

'As *hanchō* you technically have to volunteer for the fire brigade.'

'Me?'

'Man's job.'

'Well, nope.'

'Too late. I signed your name.'

'You signed my name?'

'Don't worry, you won't have to do anything.'

'Should I say that when the fire's blazing and they demand to know where I am?'

'It'll be fine.'

'What else have you signed me up for?'

In Rainbows

When we first moved out here I was still running my own English school. I'd been self-employed for eight years, and although I enjoyed having no boss, and being able to set my schedule had allowed me to publish three novels in three years, the negatives had long since outweighed the positives: I had to do my self-assessment tax returns in Japanese, I had to spend money on advertising, I had no idea where my income was coming from each month. I was desperate to move on but after a few months of trying to pick up new students in the village, I knew it was never going to work.

Fortunately, fate came along at just the right time. One friend, finding out I lived in deepest, darkest Gifu, put me in touch with another *gaijin* about half an hour's drive from me, a guy from Essex, Ben. That first winter we met up for a drink in the nearest town, a convenient halfway point, and immediately hit it off. We're the same age, with a love of multiple genres of music, books and snooker. We've both married Japanese women and are committed to the lifetime reality of property ownership here. Ben has two daughters and his wife Aiko comes from the same town. As a result, Ben knows the area and the people very well. He's one of these effortlessly friendly people who make awkward bastards like me sick with jealousy. He gives off an approachable, non-threatening vibe and so falls easily into conversation with whoever might be around. He also enjoys gently testing people, knocking them out of their comfort zone in the name of science/entertainment.

One such attempt with me, early on in our friendship, was to take me to the Rainbow Room snack bar. Snack bars are a peculiarly

Japanese phenomenon. The term 'snack' is used metaphorically: something had between meals. They are small bars, usually run by a *mama-san*, a female owner, where men go to enjoy some time away from the wife and kids. Customers are loyal to their snacks and usually buy a bottle of whatever they drink, which is kept behind the bar. The Rainbow Room is like this yet totally different.

The Rainbow Room is run by Sora-chan, a gay man of indeterminate age (which is to say, he'd kill me for writing his real age). Japan has a strange and evolving attitude to LGBTQ+ people. Despite a well-documented culture amongst samurai for master-apprentice, male-male sexual relationships – exactly like the ancient Greeks. What is it with macho military cultures? – many people in Japan refuse to even accept that homosexuality exists in Japan. 'There are no gays in Japan' is a common enough statement to hear. Baffling then that, at the time of writing, five cities and one prefecture have recognised same-sex marriage. There are LGBTQ+ communities in Japan, but they are far less visible and far less accepted than back home. Minori works with a lesbian doctor, the first time in her career she has knowingly done so. By virtue of statistics she must have worked with others, just none that were out. I have one out Japanese friend. The majority keep it to themselves to avoid prejudice and bullying. The situation is changing, even in the time I've been here, but it's still got a long way to go.

No one told Sora-chan. Ben met him through teaching English to a friend of his. He'd been to the Rainbow Room a couple of times. We were drinking and not in the mood for last trains.

'I know a place that'll still be open.'

'Sure. Let's go.'

'It's a bit different.'

'Does it have drink?'

'Yep.'

'Sounds like my kind of place.'

After a fifteen-minute walk I follow Ben into a nondescript building that could be anything from a coffee shop to a craft suppliers. The room is long and narrow. To our right is a bar, about ten stools in front of it. A toilet at the back, a silent TV in the corner. A male/female couple sit near the door. At the far end are three women. Sora-chan is behind the bar. He's a tad overweight, a vest top revealing a touch of cleavage. His round face breaks into a smile.

'Ben-chan! Long time no see! And a friend. Oh, he's handsome.'

'This is Iain.'

'Can I suck his cock?'

Ben turns to study my reaction. This has been a set-up for his amusement.

'On a first date? Aren't you going to get me a drink first?'

It seems I have passed the first test. We get drinks and the ubiquitous bowls of plastic packaged *otsumami*. Ben knows one of the women, who owns a hostess bar around the corner. Hostess bars are the step up from snacks, financially speaking. Drinks cost much more and you are paying to spend the evening in the company of beautiful, alluring women who fawn over your every word. Off duty, her own establishment closed for the night, she is unwinding at Sora-chan's, a place where women who earn a living stoking the egos of heterosexual men can hide out and recharge. Even so, she can't help reaching into her bag of tricks and is quickly flirting with Ben and me.

Sora-chan wants to practise his English. 'Iain, are you gay?'

'I'm not. I'm married.'

'Fuck. Ben, when are you going to bring me white cock?'

Sora-chan reminds me of Julian Clary, using camp and innuendo to unsettle people. Attack is often the best form of defence, and I would assume growing up gay in Japan, Sora-chan has had to be defensive a lot. We talk about travel; he's been to the US, asks me if there is anywhere like San Francisco in Britain. I suggest Brighton and he nods, like I was confirming his own research. He asks me why I'm drinking in this town and I ask about his past.

'I was in the Self-Defence Force. I got thrown out.'

'Why?'

'Sucking cock.'

I can't tell if he's telling the truth, flat-out lying, or spinning elements of the truth. One thing you never get out of Sora-chan is a straight answer.

We drink there until after four, when Sora-chan decides it's time to go home. Ben lives within walking distance, but I'm miles away and the first train won't come for another hour or so. When I tell Sora-chan where I live he shrieks a little.

'Really? I grew up one stop along that line. You know N—?'

'Yeah, it's about five minutes by bike. Do you still live there?'

'No. No. They didn't like me there. But I can drive you home.'

'I can't ask that. It's a long way out of your way.'

'Don't worry. Just wait a minute.'

I look at Ben, unsure if I should accept or if I'm taking the piss, getting a lift home when the guy's been working all night. Ben nods. 'He won't take no.'

Sora-chan drops me at the bottom of the garden. It's a sharp, cold morning with frost on the ground.

'Thanks. Take care driving home.'

'Thanks, Iain.' The bolshie bravado, the loud mouth, is gone. He's tired, not on the clock any more. 'Come back to the bar some time.'

'I will.' I close the door.

He slowly U-turns in the road, rolls down his window as he passes by. 'And next time bring some white cock!'

New Year

Ben got me an interview at the university he worked at and by Christmas I had a job offer. As the calendar counted down to 2017 things were looking up.

When I first moved to Japan Christmas was the hardest time of the year. My family have never been the close, clingy kind – we are geographically spread out and early on in my life independence and a love of travel were held up as aspirational traits – but Christmas was special. After my parents divorced it became even more so – two Christmases! Twice the turkey! Two whole days where alcohol at breakfast is not only acceptable but positively encouraged! Double the effort from Santa!

Christmas in Japan is a weird thing. When I first came here, it pretty much didn't exist. A few of the shops acknowledged it by advertising half-hearted sales (HEARTS 50% OFF!) vaguely linked to the titular mythical birth of the Christ and there were illuminations around train stations and the odd hotel. *Come stay at the Odd Hotel! Elevators stop on every second floor and rooms are uneven.* Due to the power of marketing, over the last decade it has morphed into something of a romantic event. For Japanese families, New Year is the big thing and Christmas has become a time when the young of Japan go on dates, exchange presents with their significant others or, in the case of many of my students, spend the fortnight before feeling increasingly miserable and alone, and desperate to hook up with someone. It's like Valentine's Day times a billion. Yay, capitalism.

My first year in Japan, 2005, I worked Christmas Day and it was the only time I remember being actively homesick. The students didn't help, wanting to know all the details about a traditional Christmas. It was exasperating repeatedly telling them that we don't eat cake or go to KFC on Christmas Day. I explained how most people have turkey but not everyone. One of my friends has a family tradition where they try to never repeat an animal for Christmas lunch. Duck one year, goose the next, wild boar and so on. Thinking about all that roasting meat made me miss home even more.

Yes, KFC. This is a thing. On Christmas Day in Japan, people stand in long lines to collect pre-ordered chicken buckets. The Colonel is dressed up like a cross between Bad Santa and a child's fever-dream of a paedophile – seriously, passing a KFC late at night in December can be a terrifying experience. This is all done on the assumption that KFC is a Christmas tradition overseas. No amount of laughter or denial from us *gaijin* can convince otherwise. It all started in 1970 in Osaka with Takeshi Okawara, who managed Japan's first KFC and filled a gap in the market with lies and crap chicken.

This is not my favourite Osaka-based Christmas thing though. In 2012 an Osaka department store won the prize for 'best misuse of English ever' by advertising a 'FUCKING SALE!' Using English in marketing has long been fashionable, but an unwillingness to hire native English speakers as proofreaders or a stubborn trust in Google Translate means these kinds of mistakes keep cropping up. Tokyo famously ran a Shine Tokyo! campaign, completely failing to spot that while 'shine' in English was innocuous, it could be read as *shi-ne* in Japanese. *Shi-ne* just happens to be the worst swear word in Japanese, one which literally means 'go and die'. It was the real-life equivalent of Will Ferrell's anchorman telling San Diego to go fuck itself.

To avoid KFC-related nonsense, the following year I flew back to Scotland just before Christmas. I had really bad jet lag all through the festivities and got stuck in Amsterdam's Schiphol Airport for ten hours on the return leg thanks to a blizzard. After that I decided to grow up. Really, Christmas is for children. I am not a child and we are child-free, so Christmas is little more than a chance to torture myself with nostalgia. And as an atheist, the supposed 'meaning' of Christmas is just ancient cultural appropriation.

Japan, having been forever free of Victorians and Christians, rightly views Christmas as a shopping extravaganza, a quaint festival not to be taken seriously by any but the retail sector. New Year, however, that's the thing. Companies close from around 29 December to 4 January and everyone heads home. If Chris Rea were Japanese he'd have delayed his song by a week.

For us, that means visiting Minori's extended family. Our first New Year party in the countryside was bigger than usual. Minori usually volunteers to work New Year's Eve shifts but that year she was off. My brother-in-law is an architect and had been sent to Mozambique for a couple of years, but had juggled things so that he could be back in time for the party. For once the entire clan would be there.

The party was held at Uncle Hideki's house (he of the whale bacon), an all-day affair. Lunch and dinner, separated by a sobering walk.

The in-laws like a drink. It was one of the things that helped when their daughter brought a foreigner home. People who like a drink tend to enjoy a healthy love of Schadenfreude and we all know Schadenfreude makes the world go round. My fumbled attempts at polite Japanese and frequent foot-in-mouth moments caused friendly laughter rather than disapproval. We bonded over drink and mirth.

My father-in-law in particular is a fan of malted barley and hops. I remember on the day of his daughter Chiharu's wedding, Yoji had been told by Miyoko that he wasn't allowed to start drinking until I arrived. We pulled into the driveway just before 8 a.m. to find him standing on the tarmac, a can of Asahi in each hand, beckoning me onto the rocks like Calypso.

This year I took a case of Brewdog's Punk IPA – product of my homeland, not far from where I came into the world, and now available in Japan – and a bottle of Highland Park as ambassadorial gifts. While the nibblings ran amok with toy trains and envelopes of cash (*otoshid-ama* – given to all children on New Year's Day and an expensive tradition for the child-free) we adults sat on the *tatami* around low tables partaking of sushi, sashimi, various fried meats and Uncle's impressively large saké collection. In his retirement he has decided to become an expert in the field, mainly, I suspect, because 'connoisseur' sounds so much better than 'drinker'. He likes playing the host, and the food and drink flowed freely.

Minori's cousin is also an architect, working for a Japanese company with global reach. Over lunch we discuss Brexit, which mainly consists of me shaking my head and saying *baka* (stupid) over and over again, and him telling me which Japanese companies are pulling out of the UK.

One perk of working for a company with that kind of reach is the presents. He produces a couple of bottles of champagne, a few bottles of wine and a bottle of rum.

'Yo-ho-ho,' I say, which doesn't translate.

'Do you drink champagne?' Katsu says.

'I do, yes.'

'And this wine?'

'All wine, within reason.'

'And rum?'

'Yo-ho-ho.' Because confusion and misunderstanding have never stood between me and a line I think is funny.

'You can have them.'

'You mean a glass?'

'Open them now if you want. But you can have them all. No one else will drink them.'

'No one will drink champagne?' I looked around at the other drinkers. Beer for all, saké for most, Yoji seems keen on the Highland Park. Shaken heads.

I often leave parties carrying more alcohol than I arrived with, but it's usually on the inside, not still in the bottles. As I head to the car, nephew Haru points at the rum bottle.

'Can I have that?'

'You want the rum?' He's fifteen. I don't see why not.

'No, the bottle.' It's a limited edition rum, and inside the bottle is a glass palm tree with jewelled coconuts.

'Sure. Why?'

'I want to fill it with water and put fish in it.'

'Do you think one fish will say to the other: "This is a rum old do."?'

'What?'

'Or one fish will look at the other and say: "I can't believe I got stuck in here with this rum lot."?'

Haru looks at me the way you look at a baffled old relative who claims to have been the first human on Mars, shakes his head and wanders off.

'Yo-ho-ho,' I call after him. 'Yo-ho-ho.'

In the afternoon we take a walk. Between our home and where Minori grew up is the town of Tajimi where you can find Eihō-ji Temple. Containing two National Treasures and officially designated a Place of Scenic Beauty, Eihō-ji is exactly what you imagine when you hear the phrase 'Zen temple'. Go on, sit back, close your eyes and picture a Zen temple. Yep, that one. There's been a temple on the site since 1313 and Eihō-ji is still a place where *zazen* training takes place. It sits on a river bend, backed by a sheer cliff and a steep hill. Tajimi is only metres away, but the setting and the preservation of the temple pushes modernity in all its bleeping horror far away. You approach down a winding path cut around the cliff, passing *jizō* statues, shrines carved into the cliff face and skyscraping pine trees. The path opens out before an enormous *koi* pond over which a humpback bridge curves. On an escarpment over the pond stands a small hut of the kind I assume Bashō would have made a beeline for, notebook in hand, which is unfortunately fenced off, otherwise I'd have moved in. The beauty and tranquillity of Eihō-ji punches you in the gut, winds you as you try to take it all in. This is where we go for a walk after lunch on New Year's Day.

'Minori, did you know about this place?'

'Sure. Why?'

'We've been together for ten years, living together in this area for nine of them. You never thought to mention it?'

'I forgot.'

Countless weekends of *what should we do?, where could we go?, what haven't we seen?* unspool in my head. Before I can make my point, a cry interrupts. The humpback bridge is much icier than it appeared. Miyoko and Atsuko, Minori's aunt, are hanging on to the sides for dear life. I run up, gallantly planning to help these elderly women down. Within seconds I'm flat on my arse. The kids think this is hilarious and join us, climbing up and sliding down. Cold, wet, sore, happy – this has been a good new year.

Touch Me, I'm Sick

My enthusiasm undimmed after Minori's disparaging assessment of my decorating skills, winter saw me tackle the bathroom. Japanese bathrooms are two rooms in one: first is the wet room, which holds the bath and the washing area. No separate shower cubicle because why have a narrow cubicle when you can have an entire room? Much more sensible.

The other half of the bathroom, outside the wet room – the dry room, I suppose – is for a sink, the washing machine and things like laundry hampers and cupboards for towels. No toilet here, because that's disgusting. Toilet in a separate room, thank you.

Kingo and his mates had replaced the wet room (see the 'Shy Retirer' chapter) but that left the dry room a mess. Kingo had rebuilt half the wall and moved the pipe for the washing machine. We'd intended to change the sink as well but hadn't found anything decent. Most Japanese bathrooms have these hideous all-in-one plastic cupboard-sink-mirror units and frankly fuck that. I had a bit of time and a bit of money so the winter vacation seemed like a good chance to finish the job. After a concerted hunt we found a sink we liked and booked Kingo's friend, Kinoshita the plumber, to come and fit it. Before he did that, I had to decorate the walls and ceiling.

Excitingly, we went for paint. White and blue: white ceiling and two walls, the other two walls blue. The sink and cupboard, equally excitingly, were white.

Yup, I'm approaching middle age. This book, mortgages and paint samples. My next book will be all about the B-roads of Hokkaido.

I got the paint and tools, stripped off the wallpaper, got everything ready, tape and sheeting down, and went to bed early; a good night's sleep before the exertions of the next day was required.

I woke up. It was dark. It took me a moment to work out why I was awake in the dark. I didn't feel good. I didn't feel good at all. I needed to move. Fast. I threw off the covers.

'Fucksake!'

I climbed over Minori, just made it in time.

'What's wrong with you?'

'I don't know. You're the nurse.'

She touched my head, my stomach. 'You have a fever.' She got her thermometer from the dresser drawer, stuck it under my arm. Even in my sick state I remember one of my favourite jokes.

'A nurse is . . .'

'Yeah, I know,' she says. I may have told her it before. A nurse is writing out a report. She reaches into her breast pocket for a pen and instead pulls out a rectal thermometer. 'Damn it,' she says, 'some arsehole has my pen.'

'Yep. 38.1. Dead yet?'

'Nearly.'

A word about body temperature. It isn't constant around the world. In Britain the average body temperature is 37 degrees. In Japan it is 36. Here, 37.5 is considered a serious fever while in Britain it isn't classified as a fever until you break 38. The first time I got sick and Minori took my temperature, she nearly called an ambulance. I felt like I had a mild cold, she thought I was dying. Since then it's become a joke. I am officially hotter than her.

She gives me a pill – she's a nurse, I've long since stopped asking what medication she has me on – and I go back to sleep. I wake at half nine, a bit better but not much. Minori has gone to work. Downstairs the paint is sitting ready. I have two days before the plumber comes. One coat today, one tomorrow. Kinoshita cannot come any other day. He's fitting us in as a favour.

Balls.

Now here's something you'll immediately recognise if you have family members who work for the NHS. It may be true of health professionals in other countries, but the nature of the NHS – free at the point of delivery, available to all cradle to grave, underfunded and over-stretched – amplifies this: unless you have actually lost a body part or a diagnosis that would require a lone piano or some plaintive strings in a TV drama, then YOU ARE FINE. Stop overreacting and get to school/work. Broken bones, serious infections, near death – these things can be weathered for days because *today I was pumping a man's heart with my hands* or *an oil worker put an axe through his kneecap, actually split it into two pieces.* (The latter I actually saw for myself doing a week's work experience in A&E. I mean. Still. Holy fuck. *Right through.*) It becomes ingrained. You are fine. It's just a fever. Stop whining. Do you have Ebola virus? Necrotising fascitis? No? Shut up, then.

I get dressed. Traditional painting attire – sports socks, old jeans, Iron Maiden T-shirt – and deal with the most important issue: what to listen to while painting. An episode of *The Great Albums* podcast followed by one of the billion Pearl Jam official bootlegs. Sorted. I want to start with the blue. If I get white on the blue by mistake, it's easy enough to paint out. Dark royal blue splashed on a white wall is going to be a bastard to hide. Unfortunately, the ceiling will be white, so I have to start there. I get to work, standing on an IKEA two-step ladder/stool thing I bought Minori to reach the high cupboards.

Life for Minori and me is a procession of problems of height. She can't reach the top shelves; I get backache leaning over the low sink or work counters. I desperately want to replace the kitchen, to import units larger than those owned by the average Sylvanian Family; she wants me to stop putting things on the top shelf. I bought her the stool; she took up bouldering.

It's a little bit awkward: we've had to leave the washing machine plumbed in. I've pulled it out into the middle of the floor, as far as the pipes allow. It's not ideal, but the way it's plumbed in, I don't have much choice. I cover it in sheets and, since floor space is limited, I use it as a shelf.

I'm finishing off the last corner. Brush in one hand. Tin in the other. As I stretch up for the final stroke a dizzy spell hits me. Everything spins and then I'm falling. I am aware of every second as I tip sideways off the steps, grab the washing machine for support, hit the floor, and my head bangs off the wall. I'm aware of a spreading liquid, a warm, sticky . . . I don't bleed white, surely. Oh fuck. It's worse.

As I fell, I dropped the tin. It landed, upside down (as with toast, so with paint tins) on top of the washing machine. Hundreds of millilitres of pure white emulsion. On top of the washing machine. Did I mention it's a top loader? I didn't? Well, it is. Turns out old curtains don't hold paint the way you'd want. The washing machine is full of paint. I am covered in it. My Iron Maiden T-shirt looks like I've been attacked by an Anti-Eddie activist.

Minori is going to take the piss *soooooo* hard.

Love Buzz

One comment people made about the original columns on which this book is based is Minori's humour. She's dry, sarcastic, deadpan. I am always really pleased when people mention this. As a writer I've predominantly worked in fiction. The great thing about fiction is that you can, within certain parameters, make everything up. Each character is a figment of your imagination, someone you can manipulate, spin, add to or subtract from as the story requires. Whether you are inventing characters to help tell a story you've already planned out, or watching a story develop as you explore a character (both are valid approaches, both have their pros and cons), you are always free to make choices. *Actually, if I make her a few years older then it would mean she'd have experienced X. If I make him a rugby fan rather than a football fan, it would give the reader different expectations about him. Does he know he's being a dick or is he unaware of his effect on others?* You have a certain latitude.

Not so with non-fiction. I've never really tried to portray real people before. I deliberately sidestepped it in my novel *The Waves Burn Bright*. The book is about a real event, the Piper Alpha disaster, but all the characters are mine – none are based on real people – and I went out of my way to ensure that my characters never crossed paths with anyone real. The thought terrified me and I ran the other way. I have a lot of respect for writers like Alan Spence and Hilary Mantel who can take real people and write fiction about them. I am in awe of people like David Peace who can do that with people who are still alive, or who have living relatives. The balls on that. It's one thing to capture a personality in words when you have a blank slate, quite another when their son can turn around and go, 'Well, that's a load of shite.'

And then I decided to write a memoir. Names are changed. Details smudged to protect privacy. But everyone in this book exists, none more so than my wife. How do I capture my wife in a few words?

Her humour. That's what attracted me to her in the first place. She was, whisper it, one of my students. Not in a sick way – she's a year younger than me, was twenty-four when I first met her and we didn't start dating until she'd left the language school I was teaching at – but it did mean that we had a weird eighteen-month courtship where at least once a week we'd have forty minutes of one-on-one chat, the topics sometimes decided by the textbook, more often not.

Minori wasn't like the other female students her age. She was dismissive, sarcastic, unimpressed with anything. An anecdote that had got loud laughter, intakes of breath, or the over-the-top high-pitched *ehhhhhhhhhhhh!*s of surprise known to anyone who has encountered young Japanese women, would get a 'that's very interesting' from Minori, in a tone of voice that brought to mind a slow hand clap. If that sounds overly negative, it often was. She could be a tough student. If she wasn't interested in whatever lesson you had prepared, she wouldn't play along. She'd torpedo your class three minutes in and then sit waiting to see what else you had to offer. It was a struggle at times. But there was something intriguing about this. I'm always drawn to the unusual, the alternative, the person who stands out for whatever reason. And I was drawn to her.

The other comment readers make – almost always female readers, with a raised eyebrow and a certain inflection of tone – about Minori as portrayed in the original columns is this: your mother is a nurse and you married a nurse?

Sure, there's probably some sub-Freudian crap in there but I reckon it's the humour. People who work in the disaster professions – health workers, fire-fighters, cops, even bar staff – have a darker and deeper sense of humour than those who keep the frayed edges of humanity comfortably in their blind spot. It's a defence mechanism and a more realistic outlook on life. In Zen Buddhism it's often said that enlightenment and laughter come together, that reality is so absurd that when you actually grasp it, there's nothing left to do but laugh at it. My mother is a nurse, my father is a retired fire-fighter, and this way of looking at the world is something I grew up around. The jokes, the stories, the very philosophy of knowing the answer to the question, 'Sure, what's the worst that could happen?' was in the air during my formative years. I loved the memoirs of Spike Milligan, *Catch-22*, *M*A*S*H* – humour in the face of war, laughing at death. Minori has that in spades. Because she's a nurse, we look at the world in a similar way. We find the same things funny, things that other people think are horrific. She works in a psychiatric hospital (I swear to God the cutest thing about my wife is that whenever she says 'psychiatric' in English, she gets it wrong and invariably it comes out as 'psychedelic' – I'm a psychedelic nurse. I treat psychedelic patients. I think she'd have got on well with Ken Kesey) and when she tells people that, their first reaction is 'that must be so hard' or 'that must be so dangerous'. Minori doesn't think of it that way. She loves her job because her patients are so much *fun*. It isn't *Awakenings* or *One Flew Over the Cuckoo's Nest*. She has one patient, a woman in her fifties. Whenever Minori picks up a cardigan or a jacket to help her put it on, the woman makes bull horns with her fingers and charges Minori like she's a matador, humming something flamenco. Mental illness is a horrible thing, but her patients aren't miserable 24/7 – they are people suffering an illness and receiving treatment, not one-dimensional caricatures. That ability to see beyond the superficial – this person is mentally ill therefore either sad or dangerous – and see the reality of existence – the sad and the happy, the pain and the humour – is something I'm familiar with and something I seek out in friends and in my wife.

So balls to Freud.

How do you paint a real character? Find the kernel that to you is most real and show it in action. Simples.

This humour. It's important. It's the core of me. Literature is pretty much mine. Music came from Dad. Comedy is from Mum. Those are my three pillars, the corners of my internal world.

My parents separated when I was twelve. We stayed with my mum. Dad and I already had music, a vocabulary we could share. Pearl Jam's *Ten* changed my world, and he got into it too, still loves Eddie Vedder to this day. It was more difficult for Mum and I to find common ground. The daily grind of living with teenagers, being a single mum and an ITU nurse didn't leave time for much else. The three of us, me, her and my sister, would rent movies. We took it in turns to choose. I wanted *Terminator*, Sarah wanted *Overboard*, every time, but I've no idea what Mum wanted. Whatever made us shut the fuck up, I'd guess.

I can't remember why Sarah wasn't there, but Mum put her foot down one time.

'I'm choosing. Trust me. Just trust me. If you don't like it, you can choose the next five.'

Five in a row? *Terminator* three times, *Highlander* twice. Sorted.

Turns out she really knew what she was talking about. We had to stop the *Life of Brian* video three times because we were missing so many lines by laughing over them. Today I only have to say, 'Don't you shush me!' and we're off. My only regret about not having children is that I can never do this myself. Well, not directly. I loaned Haru my copy of *Hot Shots* (another one Mum and I shared, one we discovered together in the dying days of the Capitol Cinema on Union Street) five or six years ago and he's not done with it yet.

Mum made me funny, if I can claim to be that every once in a while. Dad built the jukebox in my heart. Beyond that there's little else that you could point at and call Iain. The original 'Only Gaijin' articles started as a way for me to try, finally, to write comic material. Every section of this book is named after a song that is meaningful to me. Music and comedy in a book. My inheritance.

Spring Snow

I've written before about the importance of calendars, seasons and the weather in Japan. Campsites close on 31 August regardless of temperature, and no matter how much climate change messes with the reality, the 'rainy season' is still considered to be wedded to the rigidities of the Gregorian calendar. There is a value system attached to weather, chief of which is cold equals bad. Those of us who adhere to the maxim that there is no such thing as bad weather, only bad clothes, are in the minority in Japan. Even more unusual are those who think sitting in the garden during a snow storm is fun.

As winter by the calendar wound down, I decided it was time for the first fire of the year. I stoked the fire pit to a healthy inferno, fed it with the remnants of pruned trees, and savoured the scent of burning cherry wood drifting across the rice fields as the skies opened and snow started falling. Warm in my fleece, ski jacket, gloves and hat, I settled down with a glass of red wine and my phone on shuffle.

There was no chance of Minori joining me. She was inside, all heaters on max, buried in blankets, watching news reports of the coldest winter in Japan for forty years. I like these moments by myself, watching the flickering flames, listening to something appropriate – Neil Young is perfect campfire accompaniment, Lightnin' Hopkins too – losing myself in daydreams. That day I was happy with whatever came on. In summer various neighbours will wander over, join me for a drink, offer advice about fire fuel and placement, just enjoy the atmosphere, the wood smoke and Mount Ontake in the distance. In winter, I know I'll be alone. The only one mad enough to sit outside in a snow storm is the only *gaijin* in the village.

But as the new year began and my first year in the village drew to a close the observer effect made itself known. First, Kensuke came over, wrapped up like he was hunting Yeti and clutching a bottle of saké. He settled down and we passed the bottle back and forth in the white silence. Soon the crunch of footsteps announced Okumura's arrival. I unfolded another chair and he joined us. Kensuke's brother Kyota was next. Then Sasaki.

Small talk passed over the fire as the bottles of saké and wine circulated. The music cycled through tracks they recognised – The Beatles, Dylan – and things they didn't – Pearl Jam, Alice in Chains. Kensuke sang along with what he knew. Not a single *samui ne* (cold, isn't it?) was exchanged. In Asai and Sasaki's houses, curtains twitched as those inside looked on in disbelief. My wife wandered out, presumably wondering if I was frozen like Jack Nicholson in *The Shining*, a new garden ornament that would thaw out in spring.

'Oh God,' she said to me in English. 'Your madness is contagious.'

'It's not just hereditary.'

Kensuke's wife came out carrying a tray and shaking her head. 'Sweet potatoes.'

Wrapped in foil, we placed them in the fire. The women left us, still shaking their heads.

'It's not so cold,' said Sasaki.

'Will you be happy to not be *hanchō-san* any more?' I asked.

'Yes. It's a lot of work.'

'Who's next?' said Okumura.

'Hasegawa.' He leaned forward, placed his hand on my knee with a grin. 'And after that it's your turn.'

'Mine?'

'Junban, ne.' It goes in order.

The music cycled on to Pink Floyd's 'Comfortably Numb'. Kensuke prodded the sweet potatoes, their tart, charred odour strong in the air.

'I'll do my best,' I said.

'Don't worry,' said Sasaki, passing me the saké. 'We'll help.'

The snow settled, softly masking the village which was silent but for the crackling of the fire and the clinking of glass.

Harvester of Sorrow

Winter is ending, and it's time to take stock of the vegetables. It's harvest time. The carrots are . . . tiny. So are the onions. They aren't much bigger than the garlic bulbs. Still, my calendar says they are ready, so up they come. The carrots get wrapped in newspaper and stored in boxes in the garage. The onions are tied in bunches and hung from the rafters, as is the garlic. There's a veritable ton of that. The balcony, the garage, all along the front of the house under the eaves, it looks like we're trying to attract the French and repel vampires at the same time. It takes all day and my fingers are stiffer than the drink I'm going to need after all this.

Asai calls over. 'Is that garlic?'

'That is. Those are onions.'

'Really?'

Men. Size matters.

春

Spring

Misty Mountain Hop

When I first flew into Japan in June 2005 it wasn't the futuristic that struck me. It wasn't the concrete, the neon, the busyness, at least not at first. I passed through both Osaka and Nagoya on my way to Inuyama, so that aspect of Japan was unavoidable, but my first impression was the hills.

I've never been able to adequately explain this, but I'll give it a go now. There is an 'Asian' type of hill. I mean, obviously there isn't; Asia stretches from Turkey to Japan and that's a lot of geology to be generalising about. But there's a type of hill you don't get in Europe, and in my head it's 'Asian' because the first time I saw it was in the opening sequence of *M*A*S*H*. If you're not sure what I mean, or haven't seen the opening credits of *M*A*S*H*, let me elucidate: the hills are squat, about 400–500m high and covered in either pine trees or deep, thick green bush. Where dirt is visible it's sandy, beige, sun-dried. These hills range in all directions, bump upon bump, stretching left and right and back towards the horizon where, inevitably, there are proper jaggy mountains. In these hills there are snakes, monkeys, guerrillas, rebels and bears. They were, to my twenty-four-year-old mind, properly 'Asian'. As the plane came in over Japan, banking and descending towards Kansai Airport I could see those hills and something chimed. 'Ah yes, Asia. I'm not in Europe any more.'

The reason I keep putting 'Asian' in inverted commas is because *M*A*S*H* was filmed in California, so those hills are American. The misconceptions we hang on to. My entire image and thus my first impression of Japan was shaped by a bit of Hollywood sleight of hand.

*

If we're going with images from film and TV, then Japanese hills in reality are far more like those in samurai films, funnily enough. Spring is the time to be in the hills, from about February to May, because that's when they come over all spooky and mysterious. You know all that low-lying mist you see in the films when the ageing samurai gazes out over his homeland, using its beauty to inspire him for one last battle against the odds? That mist that signifies the spiritual is near at hand, that there is more in those hills, Horatio, than is dreamt of in your philosophy? Yeah, that's real. When there's a chill in the air, there's been some rain recently, the sun is fresh up, and the mist seeps into the canyons between those rows and rows of hills stretching back to the mountains, there's mystery in there, adventure, destiny. It does something to me, trans-ports me in a way that no history book ever has.

You sit in my garden at this time of year, with the mist, the plum blossom, some early cherry blossom, a touch of peach blossom, the lime green of new growth across the land, and you can feel what it was like to be a samurai, a Zen monk, a peasant in medieval times, in touch with the land, in touch with the gods, in love with and in awe of your surroundings. It rains for two or three days, followed by the same amount of sunshine, repeat, repeat. Japan is gearing up, preparing itself for a new year. There's electricity in the air and it all peaks in the spring festivals, the perfect time to be in Japan. While the four seasons thing may be overdone, may be slightly inaccurate, may be nowhere near as unique as people here pretend, spring is something the Japanese get right.

The festivals today can be traced back, in some form or other, to ancient fertility festivals. *Hanami* – literally 'flower viewing' – is mentioned in *The Tale of Genji*, the proto-novel written by noble-woman Murasaki Shikibu in the eleventh century, and is still a mainstay of the calendar. For this you will need one blue tarpaulin sheet placed beneath a flowering cherry tree. Add friends and family, liberal amounts of food and drink. Enjoy. Spring is a celebration. There is electricity in the air. You can feel it crackle over the mountains, the mystery of it symbolic in those misty clouds, something primitive, something deeply human; it's something that pulls me outside in every spare minute just to soak it up. I could feel it in those hills as we flew over, I can feel it still sitting in my garden. Our origins are in those hills, in those misty mountains, with the bears and snakes and guerrillas that still roam our psyche.

First Day on a New Planet

I'm aware that some people reading this may never have been to Japan and that by focusing on my life twelve plus years in, I'm skipping a lot of the first impressions. Partly this is by design: there are enough my-first-year-in-Japan memoirs out there without me adding to the pile. Japan holds a certain type of fascination in the imagination of some people: kids who grow up watching anime and reading manga in particular imagine Japan to be this futuristic, bizarre world of unreadable neon symbols, overly polite people and weird sexual fetishes, and that's what most memoirs tend to focus on. Oh my God, the language and the fashion and the karaoke and the *kanji* and the chopsticks. It sounds cynical, mainly because it is cynical, but you quickly tire of that image of Japan. I'm trying not to come over all FNG but there is a marked divide in attitude between young people here for a year, for their 'Japan trip', and those of us who are here for longer, for different reasons, and there are fewer memoirs for us. The media tend to focus on the robot bars and maid cafés, but a walk through Akihabara is like a stroll up Edinburgh's Royal Mile: yes, this is an aspect of our culture but not the whole picture. Scotland, Japan, every country has much of more value beneath the surface veneer, and it's that that we stay for, not the shiny shiny noisy noise.

Saying that, as a contrast, some first impressions wouldn't be out of place. When I first arrived in 2005, I began a blog – a relatively new form of communication back then, and one I embraced because it saved me from writing the same email twenty times. To get my initial take on Japan, I have to travel back to those heady days of Bush's second term, Hurricane Katrina and the first ever YouTube video.

The eye-catching thing in general is the sheer number of wires, antennae and aerials. Immediately in front of my balcony are two poles covered in junction boxes, wires. Inuyama is pretty low-level – I can only see one big skyscraper from here. It looks like a small American town: long straight main streets criss-crossed with cables, bad street lighting but restaurant and bar signs blinking into the night. You walk down one street and you could be in any Western city (though the feel is predominantly American), turn a corner and suddenly there's an ancient Japanese temple. I look out my balcony and if it wasn't for the hills, I could be anywhere.

I went to Nagoya on Tuesday. Nagoya city centre was Japan-incarnate – huge buildings, neon, rivers of people washing over and around each other. When you get out into the country it's pure Japanese, with bamboo forests and rice paddies, all the stuff you expect. One minute Blade Runner, *the next Kurosawa.*

So no one is immune.

The other day a student asked me about stereotypes of Japan. She was writing an essay on the topic for another class and was at a loss. We are rarely accurate when we try to see ourselves as other nations do, erring too much into self-aggrandisement or obscurity. She was thinking about tackling the *Seijin Shiki*. Clearly, she thought, this was on the tip of everyone's tongue when discussing Japan. I'll pause here for a moment while those less familiar with Japan have a think. *Seijin Shiki*. What could that be?

Of course, it's the coming of age ceremony held on the second Monday of January. Obviously. Duh.

To be fair to her, she'd just turned twenty and this was at the start of January, so it was quite prominent in her mind. No samurai? Ninjas, geisha or electronics?

The last one is interesting, because that is a common stereotype. Those *Blade Runner* comparisons every lazy travel writer makes – lazy travel writers like young Iain. Only that's not an image of Japan most Japanese people would recognise. There are parts of Tokyo and Osaka that kind of fit that bill, if you squint and turn your head just so. It's possible to populate Instagram with images that match half-remem-bered scenes from the last time you saw the film, but then it's possible to populate Instagram with images that show how fun and glamorous and perfect in every way our lives are. Instagram is not truth. Images lie.

Japan's cyber-security minister has never used a computer.

Japan is still predominantly cash-based.

CD and DVD rental shops are still big business.

Most medical files are on paper.

Japan launched its online self-assessment tax form in 2019.

The most used piece of machinery in every office is the fax machine.

Blade Runner? Sometimes it's not even *Hackers*. Minori and I watched an episode of *Veep* recently – strangely the only English-language sitcom I've managed to get her into – and they made a joke comparing a senator to a fax machine: obsolete, a dinosaur. The Japanese subtitles changed it to a joke about VHS. Either the joke didn't work in Japanese because fax machines aren't obsolete, or, Minori's theory, they were too embarrassed to admit that the rest of the world has abandoned the fax while Japan still clings to this most risible piece of technology.

This misapprehension about Japan's technological advancement came back to me during my first year in the countryside, when I bought a new car. Because I'm fabulously wealthy I chose a Suzuki Hustler. With optional extras (massive stereo system like the one Matt Dillon puts in Bridget Fonda's car in *Singles*) it came in at just under two million yen.

I'll never get used to counting money in millions.

The dealer asked me to pay for the car by bank transfer and to bring some paperwork in afterwards. I also had to pick up an MOT certificate and take it to the insurance company. I figured I could do it all on the same day. Make the transfer, deliver and pick up the paperwork, go to the insurance company. Minori was off, so she came with me. First stop, the local post office, where my savings are.

'Hi, I need to transfer two million yen to this account.'

'I'm sorry, we can't do that here.'

'What do you mean?

'We can't do electronic transfers. You have to do them at a bank.'

'But you are a bank. You offer the same services.'

'Yes, but not transfers.'

'So how do I pay this?'

'You can take out the cash, walk it over to the bank and they'll transfer it for you.'

I stared at her, sure I'd misunderstood.

'I can take out two million yen. In cash. And walk to the bank.'

'Yes.'

'I can take it out now.'

'Of course.'

'Um. Okay then.'

I filled in a form, waited a few minutes, and was handed two million yen – about £14,000 – in an envelope. Not even a briefcase, an envelope. I put it in my jacket pocket and walked back to the car where Minori was waiting.

'What was the delay?'

I showed her.

'What the fuck?'

'I know, right. We have to go to the bank.'

'Don't crash.'

We came out the car park, waited at the lights.

'You know what would be funny?'

'What?'

'We should just go straight to the dealer.'

'Pay cash?'

'Just chuck the envelope on the table.'

'I'm not a pimp.'

'Come on.'

'Okay.'

The poor woman in the dealership had to count it. I got 21 yen change. I've never felt more like a gangster in my life.

Welcome, Ghosts

In 2015, when my novel *Silma Hill* came out, I was asked by Scottish Book Trust to write an article about Scotland and horror. While writing that piece I began thinking deeply for the first time about how national character is expressed through genre. That science fiction reflects the concerns of the era it's written in is an old idea – American SF in the latter half of the twentieth century was really about the Cold War, the rise in dystopian SF in Scotland about today, the modernist concerns of H.G. Wells . . . I could go on. But it's an avenue less explored in the criticism of other genres. The article for SBT (which is still available on their website) forced me to go further into the relationship between Scotland and the supernatural. In the process, it also made me think about Japan's relationship with monsters, ghosts and the dead.

Japan is full of ghosts. We have a shrine in our garden, put there some generations back. A little wooden shrine with incense holders and candlesticks. Ancestor spirits overseeing the home, ghosts in the trees, energy encouraging growth. Japan is full of ghosts. I don't believe in them, but I'm not moving that shrine. It's there to stay. Just in case. I *onegaishimasu* as I pass. Just in case.

Cod sociology suggests it might have something to do with the survival of Shinto into modern times. Shinto is what Europeans would call a pagan, animistic religion, with a bustling non-material world, which posits that the emperors are descended from gods and that there are spirits everywhere. It's hard for many Westerners to get their heads around religion in Japan. There's Shinto and there's Buddhism, but where one ends and another begins is not always clear. There's a strong streak of ancestor worship which suggests Confucian influence from

China – many houses have small shrines where photos of dead family members rest alongside offerings, incense, flowers. But if you ask people what religion they are, most will stare blankly at you. I asked Minori this when we first started dating to which she replied, 'I don't know, no one in my family has died yet.' The first inkling many have about which religion their family subscribes to is whether the priest who turns up at the funeral is Buddhist or Shinto.

The key to understanding religion in Japan, for me at least, is to realise that there is no theology to speak of. In the West theology is at the heart of religion and ceremony is less important. In Europe we had centuries of wars between Christians who believed slightly different versions of the same theology. Is there a limbo or not? Do the wafer and wine really turn into the body and blood of Christ during Mass? Theology is everything. The Protestant Reformation was about, in one sense, raising theology over ceremony – get the bishops, the Pope, all the gold and stained glass and *stuff* out of the church and commune with God directly, no distractions. Ceremony, for Luther, Calvin et al, wasn't what religion was all about.

Japan never had Protestants. It never had Christians. It took one look at what the missionaries had done in places like the Philippines and slammed the door, forcing Japanese converts to apostatise or die. Here, it's all about ceremony. Religion, if you can even call it that, is about public traditions. The *Shichi-Go-San*, where at the ages of three, five and seven children visit the local shrine, pray and have their photos taken. *Oshogatsu*, New Year, when everyone goes to their temple of choice and prays for a good year ahead. *Obon*, the festival in August when spirits return from the afterlife to the family home. *Hoji*, memorial services held on the seventh, forty-ninth (and so on) days after a family member passes away. I would argue that in these situations the English word 'religion' is more of an impediment to understanding than a useful translation. 'Deep tradition' would be more accurate. You wouldn't call Hogmanay, Guy Fawkes Night or Halloween religious festivals but all have their roots at some point in religion. Forget what people believe; concentrate on what people do.

*

Whatever the historical and cultural reasons, the gap between reality and the supernatural in Japan is, as it once was in Scotland, thin. Japanese horror is, bizarrely for many Japanese people, one of the nation's art forms that has spread around the globe: *Ring*, *The Grudge*, *Dark Water* (the originals, not the crap Hollywood remakes – you want an example of cultural appropriation, that's where to look). In my experience, there's more of an acceptance of the possibility of ghosts here. My first encounter with this was while sightseeing with Minori's mother, Miyoko. We were on a walk through the woods, a path that took in some very old temples and shrines, as well as rising to a beautiful view over the factories of Kani. One of the shrines we visited was dedicated to the souls of children. It was an eerie place, even without the knowledge of its purpose. Deep in the forest hundreds of tiny *jizō* statues huddled on moss-covered rocks beside a tumbling stream. In caverns carved out of a cliff face more *jizō* stood, alongside offerings such as little candies, flowers, toy cars and dolls. Little light penetrated the pine canopy. You want to make a horror movie, I've got the location for you. I took out my camera and began snapping atmospheric shots.

'Stop.' Miyoko was waving at me from the other side of the clearing.

'What? Why?' I'd never been stopped from taking photos at shrines before. Was there some unspoken rule I hadn't heard?

Miyoko said something I didn't catch. I looked at Minori.

'She says not to take photos here. You might get a photo of a ghost.'

I looked back at Miyoko to see if she was serious. She was. Part of me, the part that was freaked out by *Twin Peaks* as a kid, the part that momentarily shivers opening a door in a dark house, the part that avoids forests after sundown, lowered the camera. The other part of me, the part that doesn't believe in God but does believe in Richard Dawkins, wanted to see what would happen. When the irrational is faced with the rational, reason must win every time. I waited until Miyoko wasn't looking and took a load more photos. Nothing. Not a sausage.

*

Japan is full of ghosts in another sense: the ghosts of history. The first year I was here, while I was still trying the culture on for size, I visited the Foreign Cemetery in Yokohama. Yokohama was nothing important when US Commodore Matthew Perry (Chandler in *Friends*) rocked up in his black ships in 1854 and demanded Japan open to trade with the world. It became the foreign settlement at the east end of the country (Nagasaki has dibs on first foreign settlement in Japan) and quickly grew into an important city. The cemetery itself stands on a bluff overlooking the Pacific, a fitting spot for travellers and adventurers to be buried.

The first resident was Robert Williams, one of Perry's sailors, but he was reinterred elsewhere, and two Russians, Roman Mophet and Ivan Sokoloff, became the elder statesmen of the graveyard. Other guests include Charles Richardson, whose death in 1862 at the hands of anti-foreign samurai led to the Anglo-Satsuma War (where the might of England laid siege to some small oranges, the kind of fair fight the empire enjoyed). Another is John Diack, an Aberdonian like myself, and an engineer who worked on the earliest railroads in Japan.

None of us are breaking new ground. The roads may be new for us but others have trodden them before. That these men did what I did, came to Japan and made a life here, is comforting, their ghosts a reminder that there's nothing new under the sun, that there is safety in numbers. Whatever brought these early immigrants to Japan – fortune-seeking, adventure, escape – they know some of what I know, experienced some of what I experienced. History goes rolling along, our lives a frame along the reel. History is all around us – that's all ghosts are, the echoes of history you can hear if you listen hard enough. The bell tolling from the temple. The veils are thin here; you can almost touch them, hear them. One day we'll join them. Become history.

Scotland and Japan have had a long relationship, and that's before considering the events depicted in *Highlander III: The Sorcerer*. (Don't look it up, spare yourself that, but basically once-immortal-then-mortal-now-immortal-again-because-we-need-a-plot-device Connor MacLeod –

hey, MacLeod, get off of my ewe, as Mick Jagger so nearly sang – travels to Japan to learn magic or some such bollocks.) After Japan realised modernisation was coming, ready or not, they decided to get ready and some busy two-way traffic got under way.

A large number of foreign experts (*yatoi*) were hired to come to Japan as advisors while Japanese diplomats, experts and those keen to learn set off in the opposite direction to look, listen and learn. The most famous Scot who made it to the last days of Edo and the early days of Meiji (Edo period: 1603–1868, Meiji period: 1868–1912) was Thomas Blake Glover. Born in Fraserburgh, he was an entrepreneur who made and lost several fortunes, based himself in Nagasaki and managed to get embroiled in the armed rebellion that led to the overthrow of the 250-year-old shogunate by running guns to the rebels and smuggling some of them out of the country (Japanese subjects were explicitly banned from going overseas). The best example of this was the Chōshū Five, a group of young students from the Chōshū clan (what is now Yamaguchi). With Glover's help they went to Britain, later returning to Japan with the experience and knowledge needed to move the country from feudalism to capitalism. One of the group, Itō Hirobumi, later became Japan's first prime minister.

Glover's life is colourful, but as Alan Spence has already written brilliantly about him in the novel *The Pure Land*, I won't go on about him here. Glover may have been the most famous Scot to adopt Japan as his home, but he wasn't the only one. Isabella Bird travelled the islands back in 1878; Albert Richard Brown and Richard Henry Brunton helped chart the coastline and make it safe for international shipping; Henry Dyer and Alfred Ewing were engineers; one of the Glasgow Boys, E. A. Hornel, was here from 1893 to 1894, and his art shows he was much taken with the place.

The one thing that absolutely never happened was that an American soldier was hired to teach backwards Japanese peasants how to make firesticks go bang. *The Last Samurai* is based on fact – certainly Ken Watanabe's character is – and there certainly were military advisors like the one Tom Cruise plays, but guns were introduced to Japan on a large scale by the Portuguese in 1543 – Catholicism, no? How about these? – so the idea that by the 1870s a Japanese soldier could only just about manage to point them the right way is yet another example of Hollywood's barbarian-washing of the world beyond white America.

Anyway, there are ghosts in these here hills, the ghosts of Scots who came before me. I'll go on the trail of them someday, my forebears, and see what remains of their footprints in Japan.

I've never seen a ghost, but I did have an encounter that scared the shit out of me.

A couple of years into our relationship, Minori's paternal grandfather passed away. She got the phone call early in the morning so we went straight over to her grandmother's place to pay our respects and offer our support. Imagining the day ahead, I began to get nervous. None of my Japanese textbooks covered what to do or say in these circumstances. I'd only ever been to one funeral in Scotland – my own grandfather's – and nothing in that experience would help me here.

In the car on the way over I quizzed Minori. 'What should I say to your grandmother? Or your dad and his brother?'

'What do you mean?'

'Well, in Scotland we'd say, "I'm sorry for your loss," or something like that. What do you say in Japanese?'

'I'm not sure.'

'There must be something. You're a nurse, what do you say to relatives when one of your patients dies?'

'Nothing, the doctor speaks to them.'

No help there. I checked online. The *Japan Times* has an article on the subject but here I trip over the problem of nuance and the indirect nature of Japanese. The article, written by Daniel Morales, suggests:

If a death is a surprise or an accident, you can say そんな . . . 大変でしたね (*Sonna . . . Taihen deshita ne*, Oh my . . . That must've been awful). Even your basic ああ、そうですか (*Aa, sō desu ka*, Oh, I see) is a perfectly decent way to respond initially when confronted with the news of a death.

'Oh, I see' didn't seem quite adequate. And what do you say next? 'Nice day for it'?

I tell this story to my first year students when we're discussing living abroad. They are often – as we all are at times – terrified of making cultural mistakes and offending people. Guidebooks and TV shows in Japan often focus on stark cultural differences between Japan and other countries, a strategy that has a two-fold effect: it reinforces the idea of Japanese exceptionalism and the idea that 'overseas' is a scary place that's hard to fathom. I tell them this story to show that there are mistakes and *mistakes*. I've been to many weddings in Japan. The first time, I had no idea what was going on and made loads of mistakes, but it didn't matter – it's a wedding, everyone's happy, everyone's celebrating, a mistake in etiquette doesn't ruin the day. You'll be forgiven, people will laugh and smile, have another drink and forget all about it. A funeral is another matter. It's serious. People are grieving, and if you fuck up you could seriously offend someone.

So I had no idea what to say. Fine, I thought, I'll stick close to Minori and she can deal with it.

'What else should I expect?'

'Nothing today. We'll just stay there, help out. The funeral will probably be on Thursday. There will also be a pre-funeral thing the night before for people who can't make the actual funeral because of work.'

'And we go to both?'

'I have to. You don't have to come to the pre-funeral.'

'I will though.'

'Don't. I'll be busy and I can't look after you.'

'Okay. So today we just stay at the house?'

'Yeah. Some people will come over. We'll have food, you can drink beer.'

'Fair enough.'

We arrive, walk in and announce our arrival. We go through the *genkan* and into the living room. Her grandmother is kneeling beside a futon. Minori heads over and kneels on the opposite side of the futon. I follow her. I'm halfway to my knees when I realise what's in the futon. Her grandfather.

His body.

His *corpse*.

Laid out. He hasn't been prepared for his burial. There's no make-up on him. He's a strange colour. He's there. Dead.

I've never seen a dead body before. I had no idea he'd be there. Surely he'd be in a morgue, at the funeral home, somewhere refrigerated. Not, you know, just lying there.

I look at Minori. She's looking at her grandfather's face, chatting away to her grandmother. He was old, not in the best of health, had been in hospital for a while, so this is no surprise. I'm not following the conversation at all. My mouth is dry. I feel cold.

Why the fuck hadn't Minori told me *he'd* be there? I wasn't prepared.

We stay there about ten minutes before Minori notices my face. 'You okay?'

'Um . . .'

'It must be his legs,' her grandmother says. 'He can't sit *seiza*, can he? Go through to the kitchen and have a seat. There's beer and food. Help yourself.'

I look at Minori who nods. *'Arigatō.'* I go through to where Minori's uncle is watching the baseball highlights. He hands me a beer. I still don't know what to say to him. I try a *taihen da ne* and it seems to go down well, or at least to cause no offence. I sit and watch the baseball with him until Minori comes through.

'Are you all right?'

'No. You didn't tell me his body would be here. I got a shock.'

'Where did you think he'd be?'

'Hospital? Funeral place?'

'They'll pick him up later. You don't do this in Scotland? Have the person at home?'

'I'm not sure. I think maybe the night before the funeral. But in the coffin, all . . . preserved . . .'

'Huh. I didn't think about it. How did you feel?'

'What's going on?' says Hideki.

'Iain's never seen a dead body before. It freaked him out.'

I glower at her. *Keep this between us! Telling the son of the deceased that his father's corpse freaked me the fuck out is definitely going to cause offence.*

Hideki just laughs. '*Sō desu ka? Bikurishita?*' (Really? You were surprised?)

I nod.

'Have another beer. It's good for the nerves.'

Come As You Are

When talking to people back home about gardening in Japan, it doesn't take long before the subject of knotweed thrusts itself into the conversation. When we first moved in, there were these dark green leaves sprouting everywhere.

'Minori, any idea what these things are?'

'Some kind of tea?'

'Is that a guess?'

'Do I look like a botanist?'

They are annoying but not overly so. A strimmer deals with them easily. They pop up now and again but grow slowly so they are only a mild irritant. There are far more pesky varmints to keep me busy – lots of climbing vines that flock over a tree or bush like modern zombies over a CGI tower block in the blink of an eye. It was only when an actual botanist (well, a friend who studied botany and now runs a flower shop) came over for a barbecue that I found out they weren't some kind of tea.

'Oh, you've got *itadori*. That's not good.'

'How do I deal with it?'

'*Tenchi gaeshi*.' Hell over heaven.

Afterwards – a few days afterwards, if you can do *anything* the day after one of my barbecues you haven't been barbecuing right – I consulted Professor Google and lo! Turns out I had Japanese knotweed. Prior to this, the only time I'd ever come across knotweed was when answering the question: 'What's that you're smoking?' I'd thought the only invasive species in my garden, apart from me, were crab grass and my turtle, Lincoln.

Crab grass is a tufty little shit that gets everywhere, a bit like Michael Gove, though it only takes a good jab with a shovel to get rid of it, which might work on Michael Gove. I don't know how it spreads but no sooner have I dug it out of one section than it reappears somewhere else, a bit like . . . Lincoln is a turtle of North American ethnicity and when we bought him in the pet shop we had to sign a contract saying we wouldn't release him into the wild. The rivers are apparently full of Lincolns, aggressive hungry wee bastards who push native species out of their habitats. We keep him in a pretty prison so he can't invade the waterways of Gifu. A large plastic detention centre where he is well fed but isolated. He may have come here legally – we have a badly photocopied contract to prove it – but he's not exactly welcome.

Knotweed. Japanese knotweed. An invasive species? That can't be right. Not here anyway. It's Japanese knotweed. This is Japan. It's a native species. A pain in the hole, true, but it's hardly 'alien'. It's just a plant going about its business of survival. It's not like it's sitting around like a Victorian Englishman plotting expansion and colonisation – 'The sun never sets on the knotweed empire.'

When you dig into the subject of invasive species, you unearth a world of openly expressed xenophobia. It's never knotweed. It's always Japanese knotweed. Andean pampas grass, European rabbits, Chinese mitten crabs, Florida lionfish, the Pacific rat. It's policed by bodies like the California Native Plant Society and dealt with by government policies such as the Great Britain Invasive Non-native Species Strategy. They speak of invaded ecosystems, alien species and integrated pest management in communities while experts in invasion biology even hold conferences on interplanetary contamination. A Faragian lexicography to describe what are innocent animals moving in search of food, waterborne life scooped up in the ballast of ships, seeds carried on the air currents. It's not like the crabs paid some dodgy guy with a rickety dinghy to get them across the sea. The grass didn't spend days inside refrigerated trucks or hanging from the underside of the Eurostar.

Alien species. I have an Alien Residence Permit. I could easily take the above silliness to extremes, spin a fantasy about rabbits drowning in the Med while Italian politicians talk of a *Watership Down* future, but there's a serious point about language here. These aren't discrete areas – it'd be pretty easy to draw a Venn diagram showing the overlap of language used by invasion biologists about alien species that destroy the balance of an ecosystem and the language used by the Right to describe immigrants. There are groups of people who actively hate the grey squirrel because it has ousted the 'native' red squirrel. Hate.

It's too easy to slip into this language, these categories. It infects science, an area of human activity with a long history of infuriatingly inaccurate use of language: the Big Bang (wasn't big, nor did it bang), the whole theory/hypothesis confusion (to be fair, this is more a mistake made by non-scientists who use theory to mean idea, but we're never going to change that error). Language is like a rail system, and if we aren't careful it can haul us down one specific track before we've had a chance to actually think. Invasive, foreign, these are bad things. Native, indigenous, these are good.

Whenever we talk about something coming into one area from another, the language we use means we begin from an inherently negative standpoint. Before the animal/mineral/vegetable/idea has even been considered on its own merit, we're already playing with a handicap. It takes effort to get back to neutral, long before we can get anywhere near positivity.

I see this at work. In my writing classes, one of the assigned essay topics is immigration to Japan (not my idea, this is clearly asking for trouble, but I suppose someone somewhere knows what they are doing). Without exception the students begin their essays with some variation of 'Immigration is not something we really want, but are there any merits to the idea?' That's the battlefield we're standing on. 'In an ideal world everything would stay exactly where it is, but the world isn't ideal [wipe away a tear] so let's hunt for some silver linings.'

It's all over British politics today, behind everything Trump says. It's universal and timeless. It was all over Japanese literature in the Modern Era (the Modern Era in Japan began on 23 October 1868). In the face of foreign threats Japan undertook to modernise. This wasn't a linguistic threat – the US sailed into Tokyo Bay and ordered Japan to open its ports. Gunboat diplomacy. Japan took one look at what the British had just done in China and rightly thought, We need to do something about this. Rapid modernisation of every corner of society gave the writers of the era whiplash, and while embracing the European novel form they used the country's hills and valleys to lament the passing of a native way of life. It's long been a theme of Japanese literature: the end of an era, the setting sun. The way of counting the years, the Emperor system, almost guarantees it. I write this in the first month of Reiwa, the new era under the new emperor. Meiji ran from 1868 to 1912, Taisho 1912 to 1926, Showa 1926 to 1989 and Heisei from 1989 to 2019. A generation or two each time. From coronation to death (except in this instance, when the Heisei emperor retired). This generational shift, a definitive marker between the present and the past, naturally produces a lot of soul-searching, looking back and looking forward. Where were we? Where are we now? Where are we going? There's never anything akin to the Parisian *fin de siècle*, the bright new future full of bright new things. Japan is a melancholy place, with the future only visible in the peripheral. Change is turbulent; the past static. You can see the appeal. Even the future is invasive, let alone these *gaijin*.

In Scotland, some people call the English who have moved north 'white settlers'. In rural communities on the west coast you can be an incomer for half a dozen generations. It's all a bit daft, really. We need to relax, go with the flow much more. Smoke some of that not-knotweed.

Saying that, native or not, the knotweed has got to go. I'll turn hell over heaven, at least for a weekend. Then I'll probably forget for a few weeks until I find some of it threatening a tomato plant, or my new raspberry bush, then I'll get all genocidal on its arse.

Eruption

From our garden, looking east across the rooftops, over the train line, up the gently rising hill and beyond the *onsen*, the ragged silhouette of Ontake-san holds the eye. It makes for a dramatic backdrop to barbecues, and is especially beautiful in spring when the mountain, still snow-embraced, stands in classical artistic contrast to the soft pink cherry and deep purple plum blossom. At times like those it's hard to remember that the picture-perfect peak is deadly.

Ontake is an active volcano, one of 111 in Japan. By the standards set by Sakurajima, far down south in Kagoshima, it's pretty quiet – Sakurajima erupts on average a thousand times a year. Obviously it isn't lava-spewing, disaster movie-level stuff but it is a constant plume of ash bursting into the atmosphere and spreading black particles across the homes and cars of Kagoshimaites. In comparison, Ontake is quiet. But as any geologist, meteorologist or teacher will tell you, it's the quiet ones you should keep an eye on.

At 11.52 on the morning of 27 September 2014 Ontake erupted. Mountain climbing is popular in Japan, and Ontake is a popular climb. Hundreds of people were on the slopes, many of them near the top. There are videos uploaded to YouTube by climbers who survived. They're terrifying to watch. Fifty-seven people died and a further six have never been found.

The week before, Minori and I had been discussing climbing Ontake. We decided against it. I can't even remember why, just not in the mood that week. We could have been up there.

In Japan, the unexpected can happen any time.

Gifu is considered pretty safe. There hasn't been a big earthquake in the Tokai region since 1854. Before that it was 1707. Then 1605, 1498. See the pattern?

We're due.

Each Tokai earthquake has been around an eight, seven by the Japanese scale. In short, Japan measures earthquakes by the intensity of shaking, as opposed to energy released Mw. No one uses the Richter scale any more because it isn't very accurate; it's only the media that still uses the term. The Tohoku earthquake in 2011 was a seven (Japanese scale).

We're overdue.

You live with this knowledge in the corner of your eye. In the cupboard by the door we have twelve two-litre bottles of water. Flashlights. A solar-powered lamp. A wind-up radio. A first-aid kit. We have a plan. A meeting place if we're separated. We're talking about geology here, so it's not a case of if or when – it's both. It will happen. It just may not happen in our lifetime. Or it'll come tomorrow.

I've mentioned elsewhere that one thing that exercises many of us immigrants to Japan is the idea of being accepted, of assimilation, of being treated not as a visitor but as a permanent fixture. Out here in the village it was a worry. How much pushback will I receive for being a foreigner? Kensuke's question about whether I'd die in Japan epitomised the conundrum, encapsulated the difference inherent in our position. There is always the possibility that we could leave.

This difference between us and them was never more apparent than in March 2011. The earthquake. The tsunami. The nuclear meltdown.

I was in our apartment in Komaki at the time, chatting on Facebook Messenger with my friend Mike, who was working in an office in Tokyo. I was sitting at the kitchen table, Minori was standing. An interesting thing with earthquakes, small ones, is that depending on your location, you may not notice them. I've been standing in front of class and not noticed a quake that all the seated students felt. I've been woken by crumps that Minori has slept through. This was nothing like that. It started shaking. Usually the shakes last five seconds and die off. This one didn't. It kept going. And going. More than thirty seconds. We were 700km away from the epicentre and it's still the biggest quake I've experienced. The pull cord for the light was dancing. The utensils hanging from the rack were swinging. In Tokyo, Mike typed: *What the fuck! Earthquake!*

We switched on the TV and watched the horror unfold. I kept the conversation going with Mike, hiding under his desk on the seventh floor, until the quakes subsided and they could evacuate.

As we watched, the tsunami hit. It was like watching the second plane hit the second tower – the same feeling of numb disbelief, the same feeling that in that moment everything had changed. We watched for the rest of the day. I cancelled my classes – the students wouldn't come anyway. Everyone was staying close to home, scared about what could happen next.

One scene will never leave me. They only showed it once. I don't think they'd realised what the footage showed the first time. It was amateur mobile phone film recorded by someone who'd got safely to the top of a hill overlooking a coastal town. The tsunami swept through the picture. Higher than houses. Cars carried in the wash. Gunmetal grey, a cement wall thundering across the town. In the bottom right of the screen an elderly couple were running towards the camera, trying to reach the hill. She was struggling, weaker than her husband, slower. He was helping her. The tsunami rolled closer. He urged her on, almost dragging her. The tsunami closed in. You could see him, this tiny figure at the bottom of the hill, you could see him look at her, look at the wave, turn and run. Abandon her. He made it maybe three metres before the wave took her. Another metre or two and he went under.

In the days afterwards lots of foreigners left Japan. There are countless stories across the net of people walking out of jobs, leaving everything in their apartments and heading straight to the airport. Some phoned from the terminal. Others sent emails once they were safely home. Forward my final salary. Sell whatever I've left in the apartment. Some countries arranged free flights for their citizens. These people were labelled 'flyjin' – *gaijin* who took flight.

I'm not going to judge. Everyone's situation is different, and there was so much disinformation floating around that it was hard to know what to believe. I remember watching NHK World on my laptop while watching NHK Japan on the TV. The same station was giving contradictory reports concerning the danger around Fukushima, the size of the exclusion zone, the prognosis. NHK World was much more panicky, NHK Japan clearly more concerned with playing down the risk to avoid panic. But there was some insane overreaction. A German friend of mine had booked a holiday to West Japan – Hiroshima, Fukuoka, Nagasaki, Kumamoto, Kagoshima – for the end of March. She asked me if I should cancel. I said not to – Hiroshima is more than 1,000km from Fukushima. She cancelled anyway, because German news was reporting that the reactor had exploded, that radioactive debris was scattered across the landscape. They were making stuff up, scaremongering. I told her so. She said I was buying into Japanese propaganda. I got angry. We haven't spoken since.

We know now how much the government and TEPCO (Tokyo Electric Power Company) were keeping from the public. We also know how much nonsense was being spread. Conspiracy theory after conspiracy theory obscuring the real conspiracies going on. With hindsight, the people who left overreacted. With hindsight. Some came back, embarrassed, sheepish, to find that their jobs hadn't been kept open for them, that their flats had been re-let, their possessions sold or dumped. They returned to derision from those who had stayed.

I won't judge, but I will say this: you don't get to demand to be treated the same as native residents if you run off at the first sign of danger. Japanese people can't do that. Every earthquake, volcanic eruption, nuclear meltdown has to be survived. To assimilate, to become part of your adopted home, you need to be there for the bad as well as the good. You don't qualify marriage vows with an asterisk after 'till death do us part'. Leave, by all means, but your complaining privileges have been revoked.

If you have one foot out the door, you can't be surprised if people question your commitment.

Greet Death

In 2005, just before I came to Japan, I went to visit my maternal grandparents to say goodbye. They had recently moved from the big house in the middle of the forest I previously mentioned to a bungalow in a nearby town. They were getting on a bit, my grandmother had recently been hospitalised and being so isolated wasn't an option any more. We'd always lived within a few miles of them (my father's parents lived in Ayrshire) so my sister and I had always been a touch closer to them. We had the usual cups of coffee, oatcakes and cheese, my granddad cracked jokes, and my grandma told me how people I'd never heard of were getting on. As we left my grandma took me aside.

'Listen. If either of us dies while you're out there, don't come back.'

'Oh no, don't say that. Of course I'd come back.'

'No. It's daft. It's a long way and must cost a fortune. I won't mind. I'll be long gone anyway.'

Mortality was clearly weighing on her mind. It had been for some time. It had become a family joke as far back as I can remember that whenever the whole clan was together we'd have a group photo because 'it might be the last chance we get'. Rolled eyes, shaken heads. Dinnae be daft.

They were fighters. First Hitler, then the Grim Reaper. My grandfather was in the RAF during the war. I stole the facts of his war and gave them to my fictional pilot, Jack Devine, in my first book *First Time Solo*. His experiences were nothing like Jack's, but his logbook, his dates, his stories were the scaffolding on which I hung a story about male friendship. In reality he spent most of the war training in Canada. He never saw combat, and when, as kids, we asked the inevitable, 'What did you do during the war?' he said, 'I hid.'

My grandmother probably had the more interesting war. She was a WAAF in the Pathfinder Force, one of the most important branches of Bomber Command. She knew and worked closely with all the key figures. She was also into amateur dramatics, and there are photos somewhere of her onstage in a Noël Coward play.

In 2005 neither was ready to give up. I was only going for a year. What were the odds?

In 2008, after a year back in Scotland, Minori and I decided that our life in Japan was better than a potential life in Scotland. Just logistics – work, income, security. This time the odds of someone dying while I was on the other side of the world were much higher. The highest, in fact. One hundred per cent certainty.

Grandma got worse. Went into a home. She was there for years. Every time I went back we visited. Formerly a force of nature, she got smaller, thinner, weaker. I saw her on average every year or two. The change was noticeable each time. There were a number of false alarms. My granddad was doing fine. His memory wasn't what it was but physically he was strong. Swimming every morning. Staying healthy to look after his wife.

In 2017 she passed away. Nine months later, my grandfather followed, as we knew he would. After more than sixty-eight years together, they couldn't bear to be apart. As promised, I didn't go back. Instead I held my own wake, lighting a fire in the garden, sitting there with Ontakesan proud on the horizon, thinking about the influence they had had on me, letting the memories flood back. In some way the kernel of this book started around that fire.

I don't like dwelling on the past. At family gatherings when someone gives it, 'Do you remember when . . . ?' I get all itchy and ready to leave. The future is far more fascinating than the past. The past is done. The future is full of possibility. But this time I didn't fight it. I let the subatomic strings connect the past with the present. I was sitting in my own mini forest because that's where I felt comfortable. That's what home meant: trees, fallen leaves on the ground, seasonal change. Everything we'd listed to the *fudō-san* were things I'd taken from my grandparents and my parents (my mum grew up in that house, my father heavily bought into that world). The smell of woodsmoke was home. The hammering of the woodpecker, the splash of the fish catching insects, the *gero* of the frogs at night, they are what makes somewhere home. I'd travelled to the other side of the globe, as far east as I could go before coming back, and had tried to build a little piece of Aberdeenshire in Japan's green and pleasant land.

I was at work when my father phoned, between classes so I answered, but very quickly I had to tell him I'd call back. I knew something was wrong. Dad doesn't phone. He sends one-sentence emails every few weeks or so. I think he's used Skype once.

The future is full of possibilities.

Bladder cancer.

There's a moment you realise your parents aren't immortal. It comes as a child, and I don't remember it. There are seasons of life, stages you pass through like the tail of a comet. Suddenly everyone's getting married. Now everyone has kids and can't hang out. Now people are getting divorced and can hang out again. Now your grandparents are all dead and your parents are getting cancer.

The highest, in fact. One hundred per cent certainty.

Dad got treatment and is now fully recovered. But it's an extinction-level event, a hard line in the sediment that I can point at, archaeologist of myself. The moment when the sentence 'At some point my parents will die' stops being hypothetical and becomes something that needs to be thought about. That needs to be planned for. It's all very well my grandma making me promise not to come back for their funerals, but a solitary wake with a bonfire and a bottle of Talisker isn't going to be enough. There's going to be a point where I need to book myself on the next flight out.

I called my sister Sarah. She lives in London. 'Listen, we need to talk about this.'

'Yeah, I've been thinking about it too.'

'I'm going to need to rely on you for the phone call. You know what I mean? You're the one who's going to have to make the judgement: Iain, get on a plane.'

My dad's sister Kathleen emigrated to Sydney years ago. We saw the way it was handled with her when my dad's parents died. A false alarm and you might not get a second chance. A false assumption that they'll pull through and you don't get to say goodbye.

Tag, Sarah, you're it.

I meet Ben. 'Yeah, I've had the same conversation with my sister.'

I meet Luci. 'My mum's already deteriorating. I need to move back and look after her.'

I know I've had it easy. I know I'm blessed. I have friends who have already lost one or both parents. Friends who never knew a parent. As an emigrant I'm blessed. I left through choice, I didn't leave people behind under a brutal dictator, starving in a famine, massacred in a war. I didn't have to cross oceans on a raft, cling to the underside of trucks, walk for weeks and weeks just to be caged when you arrive. I've had it easy. But there isn't a league table of suffering. One person's suffering doesn't negate another's.

There are few things more universal than the knowledge that one day you will bury your parents.

When my dad was out in the October of our first year in the village we talked about it. How he wanted to go. His funeral. Which music he'd want played.

'Catherine wants "Always Look On The Bright Side Of Life",' he said. 'Funnily enough, so does your mother. There must be something about me.'

And then he surprised me.

'How about you? If you die out here. Before us. Where do you want buried?'

To buy time, I steal a joke from Jeremy Hardy. 'I want to be scattered. Not cremated, just scattered.'

'Seriously.'

'Here,' I say. 'In my garden. Under the cherry blossom, looking at Ontake-san. Scatter me here.'

The Snow It Melts the Soonest

In physics, there is the concept of the observer effect. It states that the act of observation will necessarily alter the thing being observed. You can't check the pressure of a tyre without some of the air escaping. Immersing a thermometer in a liquid to measure the temperature will change the temperature of the liquid. Pointing a camera at someone automatically causes them to suck in their stomach. Observation changes the observed.

Moving to rural Japan has changed me. Of course it has; it couldn't not. I've become calmer, more patient. Things happen at a slower pace here, or not at all. Like it or not, you have to wait. Convenience is an afterthought. Mick Jagger could very well have been thinking about the lack of convenience stores in rural Gifu when he penned 'You Can't Always Get What You Want'. I've developed a new skill set. I've learned how to grow vegetables, how to bring down rotten trees without endangering all life in the vicinity. I've been inducted into the secret ways of the community association and have come to understand the importance of appearance over reality in dealing with social expectations. The Iain of Scotland Past wouldn't recognise the Iain of Japan Present, and not just because of the effects of ageing, cell regeneration and the addition of a beard you could lose a badger in.

But the observer effect states that while I've changed under the gaze of my neighbours, they must have changed as I've been observing them. Another law in physics states that for every action, there is an equal and opposite reaction. The mere presence of a foreigner amongst them must have had some impact, however small.

Saying that, in April 2019, the day before the spring festival at the local temple, Minori and I took an evening stroll down to look at the cherry blossom, lit up in the darkness, a rare event since the village doesn't usually have the money to afford such extravagances as that. The drummers were running through their routine for the next day and a couple of old men were just hanging around, enjoying the atmosphere. A couple sidled over to us.

'Hi. Do you speak Japanese?'

'I do. It's a nice evening, isn't it?'

'It's beautiful. Where are you from?'

'Scotland. Do you know it?'

'I do,' the other man said. 'I was once sent to Glasgow on business.'

'Oh, what business?'

'Sales. Nothing interesting. I'm retired now.'

'Can I ask,' the first one said, 'why are you here? How did you know about this temple?'

'We live over there,' I said, pointing to our house five minutes' walk away.

He looks confused. Looks at Minori because I must have made a mistake with my Japanese.

She concurs. 'That's us.'

'Eh? Did you just move in?'

'Three years ago.'

He looks shocked, stricken. 'I had no idea.'

Country Feedback

Inakamono they call it here. Country bumpkin. Hillbilly. Teuchter. Surely every language has a word that defines the status gap between urban and rural, or an image, be it Worzel Gummidge or a toothless banjo player. In Japan, it's often the clothing or the cars that mark you out. Ideas of fashion and style that are a couple of years out of date and done on the cheap, too colourful, garish, gaudy. 'Look at the way he's dressed! *Inakamono!*' More often it's age. Cities are reserved for the young: leaving their parents, their grandparents behind on the family plot, visiting at New Year, in Obon (a holiday period in mid-August), kids amazed at the space, bored by the monotony. At what point in the history of humanity did this split take place? Who were the first city-dwellers to gaze askance down their nose at their backwards cousins out in the sticks? Has it always been this way? Did one of the first cities get its name from the sound residents made when they peered over the walls at the peasants: *Ur.* Did the first farmers look at nomads the same way?

A Simon Munnery joke comes to mind: 'There are those who live in the city, who we shall call citizens. And there are those who live in the country, who shall remain nameless.'

In October 2018 I travelled to Tokyo for a conference. As this involves a long walk to the station and then six trains, roughly five hours door to door, I went the day before and revelled in the fun and noise of the metropolis. Stepping onto the famous Shibuya crossing, I was struck first by the sheer number of people, and then by the percentage of non-Japanese faces. Lumping tourists and *gaijin* Tokyoites together, it must have been around fifty-fifty. I felt out of place, suddenly stressed and overwhelmed by the proximity of humanity, by the lack of horizon. In that moment I realised I too had become *inakamono*. At home, around the village, there is space, there is horizon, there are no other foreigners.

In Shinagawa station I ordered some ramen for dinner before catching the Shinkansen to Nagoya. I ordered in Japanese, even though the man behind the counter spoke to me in English.

'*Tonkotsu ramen no gyōza setto to bīru kudasai.*'

Pork bone ramen with dumplings and rice, and a beer please.

He began the preparation and we started chatting. After a few sentences he looked at me, amused and said, '*Inakamono!*'

Everyone at the counter turned to look at me.

'Say something else.'

'What is it? My pronunciation?'

'Yes, and your words. Everything. You sound like a farmer. No, no, no, you sound like a farmer's wife. Where did you learn Japanese?'

'I live in Gifu Prefecture.'

'*Ah. Inakamono! Gaijin inakamono!* You are the first one I've met. You are married? Japanese wife?'

'Yes.'

'She taught you Japanese? That's why you speak like a woman!'

'No, she didn't teach me, but all my teachers have been women.'

'Too funny. Hey, Toshi-kun, come and listen to this. Have you ever heard of a *gaijin inakamono*?'

The idea of fitting in. Racists talk of fitting in and adopted values, like the Borg in *Star Trek*. They mean pretending. 'Can't you just pretend to be more like us?' What the racists mean is: differences scare us. Try not to be so different.

It'll never happen, certainly not for me. I'm over six foot, with blond hair, blue eyes and a beard, broad and bulky, like a rugby player gone to seed. (A weightlifting obsessive once told me that if I took weight training seriously I could be a 'beast'. 'A waste of genetics,' he said. I never bothered asking him why I would want to be a 'beast' nor what I would do once I became one.) I chose to live in a country where the average height is 171.2cm and the default hair colour is black. Here, I stand out. I always will. Short of doing a Sean Connery in *You Only Live Twice* or a Peter Sellers in *Fu Manchu*, you will always be able to spot me in a crowd. I've stopped looking around for the people I'm due to meet. They always see me first.

So the man in the ramen shop was paying me a compliment. In a way, as much as is possible, I have assimilated. It wouldn't have been my intention to assimilate as a farmer's wife, but you can only play the cards you're dealt. I've sculpted my own niche in the Japanese countryside and made it my home. I am *inakamono* now, just as I was a Teuchter in my childhood, and I embrace it. I am *inakamono*. I am one of those who lives in the country, who shall remain nameless. I am, for now, the only *gaijin* in the village.

Glossary

Ainu the indigenous people of Japan, now sequestered into a small part of rural Hokkaido (already the most rural part of Japan). As with most indigenous peoples, their story is horrific and heartbreaking. To put it into context, a bill to officially recognise the Ainu as indigenous to Japan (that is, as having been here before the Japanese) was submitted for consideration in 2019.

atsui hot. Basically a greeting in summer and the main topic of conversation until someone mentions food. Which can also be hot.

baka stupid. A guy I used to work with famously said, 'You shouldn't use this. They get angry if you call them stupid.' As opposed to people from every other country who really don't mind?

bikurishita Japanese can be quite a literal language. When you are surprised, you say, 'Surprised!' When you hurt yourself, you say, 'Painful!' (*itai*). Delightfully, exclamation marks in Japanese are called *bikurima-ku* (surprise mark). More delightfully, there is a chain of restaurants called *Bikuri-donki* (Surprise Donkey).

doko I first learned this from a book called *Making Out in Japanese*, basically a phrase book of swear words and those to do with getting, having and dealing with the consequences of sex. It offered the following helpful couplet:

> *sawatte* – touch me.
>
> *doko* – where?

fudō-san estate agent. This is one of the words that even when I'm speaking English in Japan, I use the Japanese word. Each English-speaking country has its own way of describing the job of *fudō-san* and I can't be bothered changing my vocab for each situation, so I just opt for

Japanese. This has the drawback of sometimes making me forget the English word altogether, a common phenomenon for anyone who lives in the country of their second+ language. I have a permanent mental block on the word 'beansprout'.

ganbarre often translated as 'fight', the closest I can get through context is a mix of 'good luck' and 'do your best'; said to people embarking on or in the middle of a struggle. *Ganbarre Nihon* was the slogan after the triple disaster of 11 March 2011 (mega earthquake, tsunami and Fukushima nuclear incident). I think someone could write an interesting dissertation on the underlying cultural assumptions behind the way Japanese use *ganbarre* and the English use *good luck*. There's no sense in the former of it ever being out of your control or 'in God's hands', something that historically is present in Abrahamic nations.

genkan the entranceway to a Japanese house; literally a stone floor with a raised wooden step up into the house so you can take your shoes off before entering without having to do it exposed to the elements. Traditionally in Japan you wouldn't invite someone to 'come in', you'd invite them to 'come up'.

Gero/gero the name of a famous *onsen* town resplendent with a statue of Charlie Chaplin; the sound a frog makes; the sound of vomit (probably the worst unreleased Simon and Garfunkel track).

hanchō-san the head of the community association and the etymological root of the English phrase 'head honcho'. Usually a twelve-month rotating position. Our third year in the village was our turn. I did the equivalent of 'me no speak the Japanese good' and tagged Minori.

hinomaru the Japanese flag and a perfect example of Japanese literalism: *hi* = sun, *maru* = circle. While Japanese can be a very beautiful, poetic language, it can also be disappointingly prosaic.

hoji a memorial service for people who have passed away, held after specific passages of time with the aim of guiding the departed spirit through their journey in the afterlife. Mostly involves sitting *seiza* and trying not to fidget or fart.

inakamono Teuchter.

iwana a small white fish common in Japanese rivers. Best served cooked whole over an open fire with a skewer up it, heavily salted, and ideally eaten while walking through the streets of a local festival. When the family have a barbecue by the river in summer, Yoji will catch a few of these.

izakaya casual dining/drinking bar.

janken rock, scissors, paper; a game raised to an art form in Japan and the accepted solution to all grievances. I wouldn't be at all surprised if the government use it to make policy decisions.

jizō little statues, often dressed in aprons and knitted bobble hats, that are there to protect and give strength to travellers.

kampai slàinte mhath.

karoshi death by overwork. Despite high-profile cases little has been done to deal with a work culture where people are expected to be at their desks at all hours regardless of whether they actually have any work to do. When Japanese people claim to be the hardest working in the world, they don't differentiate between being at work and being productive at work. Having worked for Japanese companies, I can assure you, not everyone at work is working.

mamushi a venomous pit-viper native to Japan and not – not, Yoji – a tasty snack to accompany saké.

Nagoyabashiri a Nagoya driver. When you update your licence card in Japan, you have to sit through a lecture. One retired policeman told me that drivers marked as being from the Nagoya area (the area of car registration is part of the number plate) are targeted by police when seen in other areas. The home of Toyota is also home to some of the worst drivers in the world. Only yesterday (as I write this) I was at the lights next to a man playing a driving game on a PSP while driving. He didn't stop playing as he pulled away.

ohayo good morning (casual). Any connection with a US state is coincidental.

onegaishimasu no exact equivalent in English; a polite and ubiquitous way of requesting a favour or some kind of service. 'Onegai' literally means 'petition, request, vow, wish, hope'. *Onegai ga aru* means 'I have a favour to ask'. In Japan you say *onegaishimasu* a thousand times a day.

onsen a natural hot spring. The unnatural ones are called *sento*, or public baths.

otsumami drinking without eating a snack at the same time is anathema. Order a beer in most bars and you'll get a bowl of nuts, dried squid or some random morsel.

sakura cherry blossom.

samui cold. The winter counterpart of *atsui*.

Seijin Shiki the Coming of Age Day in January when, for some reason, everyone who has turned twenty in the previous twelve months becomes an adult. Why twenty? No idea. They spoke about changing the legal age of adulthood to eighteen recently but decided against it because then the *Seijin Shiki* would fall on a day when kids were studying for their exams. Fair enough. Twenty means that technically you can't drink alcohol until you're partway through your second year at uni. As a university teacher with first year classes on a Monday morning I can confirm that no one pays any attention to this law.

seiza sitting on your knees with your legs tucked under you in the traditional Zen manner. A form of torture invented for foreigners at *hoji*.

Shinkansen Bullet Train.

shōchū a liquor not to be confused with saké. Sometimes described as 'Japanese vodka', each area has its own version distilled from things like sweet potato. An acquired taste, I've found, and the bringer of hangovers.

shoganai There's no other way, as Blur once sang. It can't be helped. Tough shit. Deal with it.

taberaremasu ka Can you eat this? The bane of the foreigner in Japan. One of the side effects of the media's obsession with Japanese exceptionalism is the idea that only Japanese people can, will and ever have eaten such unusual foods as rice, noodles, fish and fried chicken.

taihi fertiliser.

tatami Those straw mats they put on the floors.

Teuchter inakamono.

wakarimashita I understand.

wakarimasen I don't understand. Highly useful in awkward, troublesome or legalistic situations, though the ethics of pleading ignorance is a constant debate amongst *gaijin* in Japan.

yukata a thin summer kimono. Not to be confused with Yutaka, a friend of mine and a mistake I make every single time we're out drinking.

Acknowledgements

The Only Gaijin in the Village began as a column on www.gaijinpot. com in May 2017 and ran for twelve months. My thanks to Jeff Richards for taking an initial punt on a roughly sketched idea, and great appreciation to Victoria Vlisides for her support and help in the transition from column to book. The original columns are still available on the website though some changes have been made in preparing this book. The chapter 'Too Raging to Cheers' appeared in a different form in *From Glasgow to Saturn 19* (January 2011).

While everything in this book happened, in some cases names, locations and obvious identifying aspects of character have been changed to protect privacy. This is a memoir, not a definitive, objective history, and as such represents my interpretation of events.

Respect and appreciation to Neville Moir, Alison Rae, Jan Rutherford, Fiona Brownlee and all at Polygon; to my Beta Readers Thom Day, Darius Fagan, Ben Filer, John Lee, John Littlefair-Molin, Stephen McQueen, Francis Mackin, Jon Todman and Kei Tsuzurahara.

For support literal and figurative, I'll always be grateful to Pat Inglis, Michael Maloney, Sarah Maloney, Miyoko Ito, Yoji Ito and the rest of the Ito clan.

Special thanks to Judy Moir for believing in me and in this book.

Minori, for putting up with all of this.